CLEVELAND TV Tales

Stories from the Golden Age
of Local Television

Mike & Janice Olszewski

GRAY & COMPANY, PUBLISHERS
CLEVELAND

Gray & Company, Publishers
www.grayco.com

Library of Congress Cataloging-in-Publication Data
Olszewski, Mike, 1953-
Cleveland TV tales / Mike and Janice Olszewski
pages cm
Includes bibliographical references.
ISBN 978-1-938441-57-8
1. Television broadcasting—Ohio—Cleveland—History.
2. Television personalities—Ohio—Cleveland—History. I.
Olszewski, Janice. II. Title.
PN1992.783.C54O68 2014
384.55'40977132--dc23
2014033433

ISBN: 978-1-938441-57-8
Printed in the U.S.A.
1

This book is dedicated to the memory of Andrew J. Kopkas, a gentleman in the truest sense of the word. We'll always remember him for his great inner strength and the highest standards of fairness, morality, and justice.

Contents

Foreword

by Dan O'Shannon

ONE OF THE ODDER things I've collected over the years is a reel-to-reel audio tape that contains sounds from a broadcast day on WJW-TV, Channel 8 in Cleveland. The actual date is probably impossible to figure out because newscasts are omitted and some of the sound was recorded over. I can only narrow it down to 1957.

The first thing we hear, once we've threaded the flaking tape onto a clunky vintage player, is some of the Jimmy Dean morning show, syndicated on CBS. We get some ads, station IDs, and then 1957 abruptly disappears, recorded over by some kids playing with a tape recorder. This lasts until a loud *ch-chunk* announces the end of the re-record, and we find ourselves back on Channel 8 and in a long section of . . . music. This is orchestral music, the kind that parents would have listened to. It took me awhile to realize that the station was just playing records to fill time in the afternoon, while Mom did her housekeeping. God knows what was on the screen—some bucolic image? A slide show? The station's logo? Did they just show the record spinning away, spreading vertigo throughout Cleveland?

The best part is when the record skips for a full six minutes before anyone realizes it and nudges the needle. Occasionally an announcer intones a WJW public service announcement. (In one, they urge kids to watch the skies and report any unusual planes to the authorities! Go Cold War!) They also play a promo for a new kiddie show, Cartoon Carnival, which will be introduced by Cleveland's newest kids' show host, Mr. Banjo—a fellow named

Don Herbert, who tells us we'll have fun and we'll "draw our pets, right on the air!"

But it's the record skip that fascinates me. In today's world, virtually every second of television programming is overproduced, the result of too many cooks, all too aware that every minute means money. It's a breath of fresh air to hear such a random, careless mistake. In 1957, Cleveland television, barely ten years old, was bumbling around, still trying to find itself. On some days, apparently, it gave up the struggle entirely and reverted back to being radio.

On another recording I have from six years later—six hours of audio from WEWS-TV, Channel 5—local shows are more polished, even if they seem all over the map. Ever heard of Telecourses? Back then you could actually take college courses over the television. Clearly, television was the wall against which everyone was heaving spaghetti, trying to see what would stick. And speaking of all over the map, that same year—1963—WJW launched Jim Doney's *Adventure Road,* where you could watch silent vacation footage narrated by the filmmaker. This simple show—for most of its run five days a week—lasted twelve years. That's one year longer than warhorses like *Cheers* and *Frasier.* It was definitely a different time.

With the clarity of hindsight, we might laugh at some of the things they came up with, but remember, these people were inventing a new medium, making it up as they went along. This book invites you to revisit some of these pioneers, a community of inspired, dedicated, artistic, lucky, and just plain insane human beings whose fate it was to mold Cleveland television—and in a very real way, those of us who watched it—for years to come.

Some of you might have this memory: Back when you turned off the television set, the picture would collapse into a glowing dot that would burn in the center of the screen for a while before vanishing. As little children, we would scramble up to the screen and look into that dot, trying to grab a few more precious seconds of TV before it was gone.

For those of you who are new to the past, welcome. And from those of us who remember it, thanks to the Olszewskis for giving us one more look into the fading dot that was early Cleveland television.

When TV made its way to Cleveland homes, the nightly family gathering shifted from the dinner table to in front of the tube. *National Archives and Records Administration*

Preface

The First TV Generation

WE ARE PROUD TO say we are members of the first TV generation. There weren't as many programs back then and, as far as we were concerned, color TV was science fiction. The pictures were grainy and black and white; you had to wait until the tubes warmed up, and whoever was closest to the dial was the remote control. We started and ended the day with the national anthem and then a test pattern . . . and it was the coolest thing ever!

In the early days of TV everything was new. It was like a baby taking its first steps. You just watched and were amazed at what you saw. It was a different life in the '50s and '60s. Newspapers and mail came twice a day, and during the Christmas season you even got mail on Sundays! You dried your clothes outside by hanging them out on a line, and you said hello to the garbage man, who picked up the can in the backyard and brought it back after he dumped it. Most homes had incinerators to burn trash, and if you didn't get to the supermarket by six o'clock in the evening, you were out of luck. Young people today wouldn't recognize telephones. We had dial tones, party lines, and phone numbers that started with letters for exchanges like Longacre or Washington. People still read books and wrote letters. Then all of a sudden the new radio sets were showing pictures. They were called televisions, and they were expensive, so you usually had only one per house. If Dad was home and the ballgame was on the same time as *Shenanigans*, Stubby Kaye took a back seat.

Special effects didn't exist yet. The people on television had to be really creative, and we viewers had to use our imaginations, too. Folks like Barnaby, Captain Penny, Ghoulardi, Woodrow, and

Dorothy Fuldheim were bigger than life. It was a great time to be a kid.

We want to make it clear that this is not a history book. Let's call it a visit with old friends, with lots of stories you may not have heard before. Writing this book gave us an opportunity to revisit a really exciting time in our lives. We hope it does the same for you. So get ready to visit a different time and place.

Back then, we viewed the world in shades of gray, and TV helped shape our lives in ways we never realized. The people we saw every day became part of our families. You knew that Dorothy Fuldheim would be there for us around dinnertime every night, and Paul Wilcox and Gene Carroll when we got home from church on Sunday. You try to describe the effect they had on us to out-of-towners and they just can't relate. That's fine. These are our special memories. So many of those early TV pioneers have left us, but as long as we keep talking about them and how much they meant to us, they will never really be gone.

—Mike and Janice Olszewski

The early days of Cleveland TV saw massive cameras and stage lights that were so hot they could bake a cake. KYW's Tory Occhipinte, Forest Fraser, Ralph Schneider and Matt Konopka compare notes before air time. *Cleveland Press, author's collection*

After the Test Pattern

When TV Was Brand New

IT'S HARD TO BELIEVE that TV wasn't always there. Most homes today have one in just about every room, and you can pick it up on your phone or computer. It was an idea long before it became a reality. There was talk about television as soon as radio hit it big in the 1920s, but the Depression and World War II put it on the back burner until the mid-to-late '40s. It's actually a pretty young medium. New York, Philadelphia, and a handful of other cities had it before Cleveland. Not much before, but when the first Cleveland stations got underway they showed the rest of the country just how creative Northeast Ohio could be.

The first station out of the box was WEWS back in 1947. December 17 at 8 p.m. It was a Scripps-Howard station, the same company that owned the *Cleveland Press*. It's still owned by Scripps, one of the few stations across the country with its original owner. The first image sent over was called a test pattern. It was a picture of an Indian head with a bunch of circles, and it stayed on long enough for the folks at home to adjust their sets for clarity. That's the way the broadcast day started every morning into the 1960s. Local TV's opening night showed a few Browns clips, a travelogue, and Jimmy Stewart hosting the *Cleveland Press* Christmas Show from Public Hall . . . and very few people could see it. There were only three hundred sets, and most of those were in neighborhood bars and store windows. More people saw it live inside the hall. Not only that, there was no paperwork showing the exact time the station went on the air. In fact, there are no logs that show the station even went on the air the next day. Plus, no one had had the presence of mind to film the debut. The black-and-white film

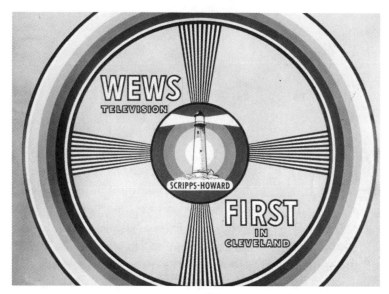

The WEWS test pattern reflects its pride in being the first TV station to make it onto Cleveland airwaves. *Cleveland Press, author's collection*

WEWS uses to show its first moments is actually a recreation done some time afterward.

Some of the names of the first TV hosts are forgotten today. Thirty years after the first Cleveland broadcast, Bill Hickey of the *Plain Dealer* would remember a typical day starting with a test pattern at 1 p.m., followed by a former Cincinnati radio personality named Paul Hodges. Stan Anderson at the *Press* called Hodges "a cross between Charlie Chaplin and Groucho Marx," and he would eventually host everything from sporting events to game shows. He also did a lot of "man on the street" interviews because they were cheap, filled plenty of time, and everyone had an opinion. Anderson said Hodges was "a sort or rugged individualist," and "anything could happen when he worked in front of a camera or mic." Some of his shows were just downright silly. One was *Dress and Guess*, where Hodges appeared before a panel of contestants in his long johns. Then he would dress in the style of a famous person, and

That's not a dressing room. Paul Hodges hosted a game show on WEWS that had contestants trying to figure out what famous person he was portraying before he was fully dressed. *WEWS*

the panel would try to guess who he was. He also hosted *Arriving or Leaving*, the words he shouted out to people at the Greyhound station as they ran to a bus. Many of the bums who took residence at the station at that time didn't like the invasion of their privacy. They relocated to the train station for some relative peace and quiet. Hodges would sometimes forget the city he worked in and sign on and off the air with "WEWS, Cincinnati." Station officials would correct him on a regular basis, reminding him he worked in Cleveland. Acting surprised, he would reply, "Of course this is Cleveland. Where do you think it is? Cincinnati?" Hodges would eventually return to the Queen City.

A few other programs filled time until 4:30, when the test

pattern reappeared for the crew's dinner break, and then it was back on the air at 8 p.m. for a very limited evening schedule. With so few TV sets in operation, any programming was seen as new and different. So were the working conditions. The station's klieg lights were so hot that the *Plain Dealer's* George Condon said, "Performers came out of the studios after a program gasping like men who had just staggered in from a cross-country bird walk across Death Valley."

When it first went on the air, Channel 5 hired a sales staff and hit the wall right away. How can you sell ad time when no one had a TV? The commercials were only five dollars a spot, and most people thought that was five dollars you threw out the window because no one would see the ad. A lot of people still didn't understand the whole concept of television. One woman got through to the general manager at Channel 5 asking how to get the pictures on her radio.

Keep in mind that at this point everything was a first, and there was a big learning curve. WEWS only had programming for a few hours a night, but the first folks to sign on had a mission, and a lot of the people hired then stayed for a long time. Betty Cope, Linn Sheldon, Earl Keyes, Alice Weston—they were all pioneers. Cleveland hangs on to its heroes, too. They all stayed in television until they got old and retired. You sure don't see that nowadays.

Television had some PR problems, too. There were urban legends (probably started by radio people) that TVs were high-voltage receivers that would send out gamma rays to sterilize you. If you were lucky your set might just explode. Also, people wouldn't pay attention to what they were doing; they would miss the ashtray and flick cigarette butts on the furniture, burning down the house.

Even so, people starting shelling out a lot of cash for TV sets. If you didn't have the money, you could sponge off a neighbor who had one or stand in front of the TV store. Bars had them, too . . . like Dad needed another excuse to hit a watering hole. Some theaters, like the Milo on Miles Avenue, set up TVs in the lobby so guys could watch the game while their dates saw the movie. A fire-

The phrase "no heavy lifting" didn't apply to the folks at WNBK. Here they're lifting a massive TV camera into Cleveland TV's first mobile studio. Used mostly for sporting events, it could carry as many as six cameras and crew. Notice the "3" on the side of the bus just prior to the move from channel 4 and the new call letters, KYW. *Cleveland Press, author's collection*

fighter in East Cleveland would show up at the station on his days off to watch TV. He finally sold his car to buy a set for his family.

When WNBK (Channel 4) went on the air about ten months later, in October 1948, it reaped big rewards from the Cleveland Indians. The Tribe was in the World Series, and hotels would buy sets and open up their ballrooms (and bars) so people could see the game. The Indians were happy. Team president Bill Veeck said, "People are gregarious. They like to mingle in crowds. Once they learn about the game they'll come out and see it. Everybody knows that radio helped build baseball attendance." Other folks weren't so sure. Browns coach Paul Brown said, "I'm not anti-television, but even the persons who try to sell television to us don't know enough about it."

Others were a tad more optimistic. Elmore Bacon, who wrote for the *Cleveland News*, predicted that "a new type of video expression" would distinguish television from radio. He also pointed out that radio executives were concerned that TV would steal a good part of their audience. Bacon went on to say, "Just as we remember the beginnings of radio in the crystal set stage, we feel sure our present sense of television at home at some future time will seem as crude. Perfection of portable television, of personalized sets and the tying of quality programming to television are some of the forward steps just around the corner. Use of television in schools and colleges as an aid to education, its use in the solving of social problems, in politics, its therapeutic affect [*sic*] in hospitals and mental institutions—all are speculative possibilities for the future." He wasn't the only person predicting the future.

WNBK's general manager John McCormick saw a "telereceiver in every home" in the near future, with television heralded as a "scientific miracle of the age." He also appealed to radio fans to give TV a chance. He told the *Cleveland News*, "NBC respectfully asks Greater Clevelanders and Northern Ohio not only to lend an ear, but now an eye. Our new television station, WNBK, opens with a pledge to provide so far as it can the best in entertainment for both eye and ear.

"WNBK comes to Cleveland, not a stranger knocking for admission, but as an old friend. WNBK in reality is just a little brother of WTAM, an old and well established Clevelander. While WNBK is to have a staff of experts in the video line so far as the technical side is concerned, with [AM radio station] WTAM's Eddie Leonard, the engineer, in charge of both stations, other departments of WTAM will take on the WNBK duties as well." McCormick had a lot riding on WNBK's success.

The WNBK studios shared space with WTAM-AM and were a very expensive undertaking for that time. The equipment alone ran as high as $275,000, with another quarter-million dollars in studio construction costs. Plus, you had operating costs and salaries. Even so, TV was growing so rapidly that managers were

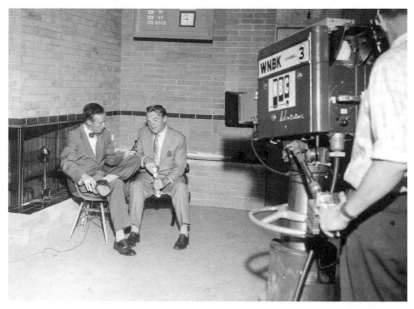

Plenty of big names came through Cleveland, and most were happy to sit down to plug their latest project. Here's Tom Haley chatting with one of biggest stars of the silver screen, Jimmy Cagney. *Cleveland Press, author's collection*

optimistic a new station could turn a profit within six months, with even bigger dividends in the years to come. They also shared a talent pool with the radio side. It wasn't long before Gordon "Skip" Ward and Tom Haley had a lot of extra work.

First, a little history about Skip Ward. He made his first appearance on WTAM as a student from Bowling Green on a show called *Collegiate Party Time.* It was emceed by a radio veteran named Joe Mulvihill. After graduating in 1948, Skip stopped in at WTAM to say hello to Mulvihill. Even though Skip had just started work at WLEC-AM in Sandusky, Mulvihill persuaded him to take the NBC audition. He got the job! At twenty-two, he was now working alongside veterans—like Tom Manning, Tom Field, and Mulvihill—whose voices he had listened to while he was growing up in Amherst. Skip was now making $120 a week, the bottom of the American Federation of Television and Radio Artists [AFTRA] scale, but triple what he had earned in Sandusky. And with talent fees for commercials, an announcer could double his base salary. Skip became one of Cleveland's most recognized commercial voices, but he eventually left that job in the late '50s to be a field rep for AFTRA, the broadcast union. His replacement in the booth at what was now KYW was Phil Donahue.

Let's not forget about Tom Haley, who stayed at Channel 3 until the late 1990s. His road to a broadcasting career started in his native New York, when he went to work as a secretary for one of the richest men in the country, Robert Goelet, in the RCA Building.

Tom remembered those days well. "I made $50 a week and was miserable. One day the boss walked into the office and said, 'I've seen guys bored before, but you just won a medal.'" The boss made some calls and opened the door for Tom to get a job as a page at NBC—which meant a pay cut to just $15. But NBC also offered its pages courses in announcing; that training got him his first real broadcasting job in Allentown, Pennsylvania, with stops at WRC/Washington and a temporary job at WJW-AM in Cleveland. That led him to the WTAM audition and, eventually, television at WNBK.

Both Skip Ward and Tom Haley had duties on WTAM and WNBK, which initially broadcast between 5 p.m. and 11 p.m. Plus, they already dressed for TV. Even in the pre-television days, NBC announcers always had to wear a coat and tie while on duty, so everyone was ready and willing to get in front of the camera.

A year into it, TV programmers were finding out this television thing was a lot more difficult than they expected. The *Cleveland Press* looked at TV's first year and said, at that point, it pretty much showed "an enormous investment, and a minimum of experience." That was on both sides of the camera. Sometimes it was just sloppy bookkeeping. Channel 5 scheduled a movie called *Four Feathers*. It was a pretty good movie, one of the few that made it to TV at that time, and everything was going well. Then, at the end of the third reel, disaster! They couldn't find the end of the movie! Turns out the film supervisor hadn't checked to see if all the reels were in house because she was heading out for a hot date. This wasn't what people bought TVs to see, and the switchboards were jammed. Even so, a lot of people were still buying sets. It was having an effect on the physical well-being of its audience, too. TV's effect on the vision and posture of the young led orthopedic surgeon Dr. Arthur Shands to warn against "TV squat," a hunching over that he worried might cause lifelong deformities. He said it could permanently misalign the hips, causing "pigeon toes."

Cleveland finally got a third station in 1949, two years to the day after WEWS signed on. It was WXEL, Channel 9, and it was owned by the Empire Coil Company out of New York. They promised stars galore when the station went on the air. The stars turned out to be Morey Amsterdam (who would play Buddy on *The Dick van Dyke Show*) and the owner's kids. WXEL wanted to have a huge complex for its offices and studios in Parma. It's where WJW currently has its transmitter. They had plans for outdoor picnic areas, a day care, and an arena for pro wrestling. It was more like a resort than a studio, but when the estimates came in they put those plans on permanent hold.

By 1950, the broadcast day was starting to fill out, though some of the programming seems almost comical by today's standards. Kay Kyser had a huge following both on radio and on a show on WNBK. WEWS appealed to sports fans with *Roller Derby* at 10:30 a.m., followed by football great Red Grange at 11 a.m. and *Bowling Champs* after that. WXEL offered *Wrestling* at 11 p.m., followed by 10 minutes of news at 12:15, and closed out the night with a dance show hosted by Alan Freed. Silly programming or not, radio saw where the money was heading.

Radio stations were lining up for space on the TV dial. WERE, WGAR, and WHK all filed for television licenses, and WERE and WHK even built stages and sets at their radio studios. After awhile it became pretty obvious that the investment wouldn't have that much of a return, so they left it to the big three. WGAR was worried that TV would steal its audience, and even hired a research group that said that wasn't likely. Some TV executives still had their doubts, as well.

Tom Piskura, one of the old-timers at WEWS, remembered a staff meeting with the general manager, Jack Hanrahan, back in 1950. He was going to be gone for a few months helping Australian TV executives get their stations on the air. They didn't know if they should be commercial-free like the BBC or depend on commercials. Hanrahan didn't think the Australians knew what they were getting into. His last words as he headed out the door were, "I feel a bit like Cortez taking syphilis to the Aztecs!"

A major call-letter change occurred when Westinghouse switched from WNBK to KYW-TV, which it promoted with high-profile events. For three days starting February 13, the station released thousands of balloons at noon on Public Square containing gift certificates of $3 and $11, reminding people that KYW was at Channel 3 on television and 1100 on the AM dial. A fireworks display was staged that first evening just east of Municipal Stadium, and mobile TV units were dispatched to local shopping centers in the hope that people would watch themselves on TV.

When they first started in Cleveland, the stations pretty much set up wherever they could find a lot of room at a cheap price. WEWS was over on East 13th Street, but the management finally decided to pull the trigger on a new building at East 30th and Euclid. Plans called for a $1.5 million state-of-the-art facility, and the wheels started moving to get the real estate in January 1956. WEWS acquired one of the last mansions on Millionaire's Row from Albert Levin's Commerce Plaza, Inc., for $450,000, or $8.72 per square foot, which was a lot of money at the time. The site had quite a history. In 1883, John Rockefeller's former partner, Samuel Andrews, built one of the largest private residences on Millionaire's Row on the same site where the William Bingham house once stood. British by birth, Andrews was said to want a "mansion so elegant he could entertain Queen Victoria in it." The house, a palace with thirty-three rooms, was simply too large to maintain for any length of time, even for a man of Andrews's wealth. It

In its early days, WEWS was located above a row of stores on East 13th Street. One of those stores was the House of Television. If you liked what they were making upstairs, you could order "take out" on the first floor. *Cleveland Press, author's collection*

was abandoned just four years later and remained closed until the Bradley Feature Film Company moved in for a brief time in 1921. Two movies were filmed there, *Dangerous Toys* and *Women in Love,* but it eventually met the wrecking ball. In all the time it was at that location the mansion had only been occupied for five years.

The start of construction was a huge event. Ground was broken for the new WEWS facility on March 26th. It was led by Joe Mario Campo, an Italian-born construction foreman with just three years of formal education. He joined civic leaders and business executives to dig the first shovel of dirt. Campo won that honor because he had been named construction supervisor on behalf of the Austin Company. General Manager James Hanrahan asked Campo to turn over that first scoop of earth "on behalf of all the men who will have a part in the building of the new WEWS facilities." It was a different time, and no one objected to the religious tones of the ceremony. The superintendent of the Cleveland Catholic schools, Monsignor Clarence Elwell, asked the Lord's blessings for the project and the people who would occupy the building. The entire ceremony was aired live, and the target date for the project to be completed was early December, so the station could celebrate its tenth anniversary in its new location. Plans also called for color TV equipment and three large studios and control rooms, double the size of its former facility on East 13th Street. It had a huge power capacity of 100,000 watts and, to the relief of staff, air-conditioning. The station would open its doors on schedule the following year.

WXEL found a new home, too. It set up shop at the old Esquire Theater on Playhouse Square, switched over to Channel 8, and changed its call letters to WJW. All three Cleveland stations would stay at those same locations for many years to come.

But you still had to get the programming in your own home, and that could be tricky. Now, keep in mind that in 1957 TV was still a very young medium. It was costly, too. You not only invested in the receiver but also the antenna and the hardware needed to attach it to your roof. That spring, the *Press* ran an article on how to maximize reception of your home TV with beer cans. The paper featured the story of two Chicago policemen who cleaned and welded seventy-seven cans into an antenna for a 700-watt station transmitter set on a ginger ale bottle as an insulator with plastic line as guy wires. All this publicity gave Dad yet another excuse to sample product from some of Cleveland's finest breweries. "Hey, I'm doing it for the family!"

Doug What's-His-Name and the Early Days of TV News

IT TOOK MORE THAN fifteen years for TV news to catch up to newspapers and radio. No one really thought television would be a credible news source. That's where you ended up if you couldn't get a gig with the other two. It wasn't until the Kennedy assassination in 1963 that TV came into its own. Even so, there were some rising stars, but they had a big hill to climb.

Part of the problem came from a lack of experience. In those early days everything was new, and Murphy's Law kicked into high gear. Jim Breslin at WEWS told the *Plain Dealer*, "It wasn't that we lacked imagination or drive; it was just that none of us knew how to transform them to actuality. It was a case of 'why can't we extend the cable to the street?' or 'what if we put the camera in the truck?' That sort of thing. Luckily, we got a little better each day." It still took a while. That same article pointed out that 1948 was "a banner year for boo-boos. Many involving mixed-up recordings . . . . Sometimes the wrong music was used. Audio engineers would occasionally grab the wrong music, playing such themes as 'Happy Days are Here Again' behind film of state funerals, earthquakes or other tragedies." At WXEL someone came up with the idea to turn a bus into a remote news studio. They lifted a camera on to the bus, but it was so heavy that it crushed the roof! Not only that, there was no videotape in the early days. Most newscasts had two pieces of film; the rest were still photos. There were no news cars so photographers would take buses to events, such as dinners or speeches. It also meant most of the news centered on what was happening downtown. At one point WJW suggested photographers ride bicycles to cut down on bus fare, but that idea was shot down pretty quickly.

That's not to say that stations didn't try to make news work. Dorothy Fuldheim had a pretty loyal following, but plenty of other people came and went. For a long time Warren Guthrie was your "Sohio Reporter" but, like Sohio, his name is pretty much forgotten today. Old-timers remember Tom Field, who was on both KYW and WEWS. This guy had a long day. He did double duty at KYW radio in the early afternoon, then ran down the hall for a full day on TV that ended after 1 a.m. But because it was late, the management let Tom do the news in a very informal manner. Tom would do some headlines and then talk about the news over a cup of coffee with some guests. He got some press, too. In the summer of 1957 Tom had a U.S. Marine captain on the show to introduce him to some single women. The soldier hooked up with one, they got married, and the *Cleveland News* called Tom "Cupid," pointing out he was "one of Our Town's most eligible bachelors." He would stay that way, too. In less enlightened times the public would not have accepted a gay anchorman.

It wasn't easy convincing experienced news people to try television. In fact, some of them had one-page resumes and still landed behind the anchor desk. Pete French was one of them. He was forty-three when he arrived in Cleveland to replace Tom Field, who was heading to Philadelphia. Granted, French had a few years in radio news, but he had a lot more in entertainment. He had started out as a song and dance man in vaudeville and eventually moved on to work at WFBM radio in Indianapolis with Garry Moore's sidekick, Durwood Kirby, on a hillbilly music show called "The Chuck Wagon." Kirby didn't have much faith in French and told him to "get out of music" and find another gig in broadcasting. Next stop was news. He and wife Linda became news gypsies, working from town to town. French met her when they were both in vaudeville, so she was used to traveling for work. By the time

French got to Louisville he had his news chops down and covered some high-profile stories, which brought him to the attention of KYW. But even in 1957 TV news could be a meat grinder. French turned out to be a very competent newsman, but if the management didn't like you, there was the door. It wasn't long before Pete French got a job more suited to his interests: singing and playing guitar at the Encore Room bar in Shaker Heights.

Primitive as it was in those days, Cleveland was still a breeding ground for network talent. Carl Stern, Jack Perkins, John Dancy, and Tim Conway all got their big break in Cleveland. In fact, for a few weeks Tom Snyder was the news anchor at Channel 3 before heading to the network and the *Tomorrow Show*. He would later say the only thing he really remembered about his time in Cleveland was Pat Joyce's Tavern, and even that was hazy. Sometimes the stations would work on image. Carl Stern had this boyish look, so Channel 3 had him wear glasses even though he really didn't need them. The problem was, they reflected glare from the studio lights. No problem. Stern just wore the frames, but he thought it was silly. Once during a newscast he reached in through the frame to scratch his eyelid. If anyone noticed, they never called the station. Later on, when Stern went to NBC, he became the first reporter to successfully sue the FBI under the Freedom of Information Act.

By 1965 TV was battling newspapers head on. That spring a *Plain Dealer* copy editor named Robert Manry decided to fulfill a lifelong dream. He took a 13-foot boat named *Tinkerbelle* to Falmouth, Massachusetts, and planned to sail it to Falmouth, England, 3,200 miles away. It would be the smallest boat to ever cross the Atlantic, and it hit the water on June 1st. Manry was forty-eight years old and in good shape, but even so, people wondered why he would put himself through this. His family in Willowick said goodbye and made plans to fly to England to see him come ashore in seventy-nine days. Some wanted to see him before that.

The biggest problem was that no one was keeping track of

Bill Jorgensen of WEWS scooped the rival *Plain Dealer* by flying out to interview Robert Manry (a *PD* employee) who was about to set a record on *Tinkerbelle*, the smallest boat to cross the Atlantic Ocean. *Cleveland Press Collection, Cleveland State University Archives*

Tinkerbelle. WEWS contacted the air force, but they didn't have the time. They had their hands full keeping an eye on the Russians. The navy, scheduled for maneuvers around Manry's route, said they would take a look and get back to them, but no promises. A submarine spotted the boat, and the news department jumped into action.

Bill Jorgensen at WEWS had a reputation for being difficult, but he sure knew to get results. He cooked up a plan to scoop everybody and flew to England with a cameraman. They hired a boat and crew and set out looking for Manry. They found him on August 9th, about 270 miles from shore. Manry couldn't believe what he was seeing. Right away he recognized Jorgensen, who jumped onto his boat with a bottle of booze, some food, and a newspaper. After Manry talked to them, Jorgensen and his cameraman jumped back on the boat he had hired, and they raced back to land. Those were the days when satellite time was in its infancy and very expensive. It was cheaper to fly back to Cleveland through New York . . . and the film even had its own seat. Manry made it to shore on August 17th, and it ruffled some feathers at the *Plain Dealer*. Photos showed him holding the copy of the *Press* that Jorgensen left with him.

The UHF band had been there for some time, but most TVs didn't get it unless they had a separate decoder box. WKBF, Channel 61, had been on the air for a few years when it decided to take on the "big dogs" and air a nightly newscast at 10 p.m., an hour before anyone else. They figured "a lot of people over forty like to hear the news and get to bed before 11." In August 1968, they debuted their show with John Herrington as anchor, reporter Alan DePetro, and a young sports reporter named Nev Chandler. It only lasted a couple of years. WKBF was losing ad money to WUAB and trimmed $400,000 in expenses when it cut the news department.

Some names stay with us because they've had such a long run. Doug Adair is one of them. He joined WJW in 1957, and folks took to him right away. He seemed relaxed and sincere, and that's exactly what Channel 8 wanted for viewers coming home from a hard day at work. The AFTRA awards named him Best Newscaster in 1959, and when WJW debuted the latest edition of *City Camera* the following year, Doug Adair was the main anchor. Those were the days when stations were willing to spend money to cover a story, and Adair got some high-profile assignments. He covered the space race and the Mercury launches at Cape Canaveral, civil rights demonstrations, politics . . . you name it, Doug Adair was the man on the scene. He also had luck on his side.

In December 1962 a newspaper strike by the *Press* and the *Plain*

Dealer drove people to radio and TV for their news. It lasted for eighteen weeks—enough to give people a taste of electronic journalism. Nine months later WJW decided to shake up its news lineup to get out of the ratings basement. KYW was king, and Channel 8 thought Adair was the guy who could topple the giant. What they didn't anticipate was the AFTRA strike in November 1963 at WJW, with their biggest names refusing to cross the picket line. Cleveland was a huge town for unions, and Adair, Jim Doney, John Fitzgerald, and others stood outside the station with signs supporting AFTRA.

Strike or not, the station still had to go on the air, so management filled in on all the live shots. It didn't go well. The station's top rated show was Ghoulardi's *Shock Theater*, and Ernie Anderson was right out there with the rest of them—between frequent stops at Seagram's Bar next door. For two weeks the station had artist Van Timmons and development manager Bob Guy wearing the phony beard and lab coat, but it was painful to watch. When the strike ended, everyone was immediately ordered back to work on a Friday night, right in the middle of Ghoulardi's show. Ernie would later say that if he had known the strike was going to end during his shift, he wouldn't have had the last couple of martinis at Seagram's! It was fortunate the strike ended when it did because things changed drastically for TV news just a few days later with the Kennedy assassination. With all the breaking live events, TV news was being seen in a whole new light.

Adair seemed pretty happy at WJW. Along with the newscasts, he was a lay minister with the Episcopal Church and hosted a TV panel show with other ministers every Sunday morning. But by 1970 he was ready for a change. WEWS approached him, and when Channel 8 couldn't match the offer, Adair signed a four-year deal at Channel 5. Some folks took shots at Adair for the move. Ken Bagwell, general manager at WJW, issued a terse statement that just said, "Doug served us well, but unfortunately, our terms [for a contract renewal] were unacceptable for Doug." No "good luck" or "nice job" or anything like that.

Newspapers and radio had a long head start on TV when it came to news, but by the early 1960s shows like WJW's *City Camera* helped change the way we got our daily information. *Cleveland Press Collection, Cleveland State University Archives*

Bill Barrett, TV-radio reporter for the *Press*, didn't hold back. Anyone who knew Bill would say he was one of the kindest and most likable reporters in town. His comments about Doug Adair were far from kind or likable, though. He called Adair a "news reader" and said that the "present news reader" at Channel 3, Virgil Dominic, was nervous. He called TV anchors "news readers" because print reporters "work so hard and write so well and scoop the electronic journalists regularly." He wrote, "Big deal! What has this Doug What's-His-Name got except blue eyes and a soft voice and a few bad jokes? What makes him worth $65,000 a year?" He thought maybe it was because Adair had "presence, or charisma, or animal magnetism, or sex appeal. Whatever it is, it is worth $65,000 a year to NBC-TV. And it has nothing whatever to do with Adair's skill as a reporter or as a writer because, like Chet Huntley or Walter Cronkite or Howard K. Smith, Doug Adair is first and foremost an appealing and agreeable performer on TV for most people." You have to admit, that was a big plus.

By 1974 he was on the move again, this time to WKYC as half of their new news team. Here's where the soap opera begins. Channel 3 weatherman Russ Montgomery was pink-slipped in 1977 and replaced by Mona Scott. Montgomery did not go quietly, telling the newspaper he was "disillusioned and discouraged" by the move. Mona had been the first female announcer at Channel 4 in Columbus before she got the Cleveland gig, and there was instant chemistry with Doug Adair. Mona was going through a divorce at the time, and Doug's marriage had ended in 1979. so they obviously had something in common. They eventually announced they would marry (after getting dispensation from NBC, which barred husband–wife teams from working in the same department). They also gave some very weird answers to interview questions.

Adair was fifty-one when they got married, sixteen years older than Mona. When he was asked by the *Cleveland Press* what attracted him to his co-anchor, he said, "She has brightness in the face. It's the same thing that comes over to her audience—her cheerfulness." Then Doug added, "She has a nice enough body—nice legs and big hips." Big hips? There was a physical attraction for Mona, too. She liked Doug's hair and eyes . . . and fingernails. "His favorite thing is for me to push back his cuticles."

Doug and Mona bought a Victorian-style wedding ring at an estate sale, and Mona's ten-year-old daughter wasn't impressed. She checked out the ring and said, "Yuck! Who'd want to wear a ring that someone else wore?" They explained the importance of the ring to the person who had left it behind and the kid said, "Yuck! Who'd want to wear a ring that was worn by a dead person?" The two got married at a church in Peninsula in November 1980 with Mona wearing a fifty-dollar dress she had bought off the rack years before in Bristol, Tennessee. It was a ratings period, but both said that was only a coincidence. Both sides also had connections to clergy. Mona's father was a minister with the Disciples of Christ and performed the ceremony, with Al Roker signing the marriage

A pair on and off the air: Mona Scott and Doug Adair made it
official and co-anchored news in both Cleveland and Columbus.
Cleveland Public Library

document. Adair was a minister, too, though his dinner-table
prayers would include comments like, "Thank God, Mona got to
the grocery store so we won't have bologna again." There was a
reception right after at the Mayfield Country Club with Channel 3
footing the tab, and there was no bologna in sight . . . but there
was plenty of ice cream. In fact, that was one of their wedding gifts.
Fellow anchor Amanda Arnold gave them nine pounds of chocolate ice cream and ten pounds of bananas. No word if the couple
was registered at Pick-n-Pay. Things were good at WKYC, but by
1983 they were moving to Columbus to take over the anchor spots
at Mona's old station, WCMH, and were a ratings magnet. The

strain of the job apparently got to them, and the marriage on and off the air dissolved in 1990.

Newsrooms are like MASH units. You can only see so much death and despair before it gets to you, so there tends to be a lot of dark humor. Stella Walsh, an Olympic athlete, was almost considered a saint in the Slavic Village neighborhood. If you were sick, she was at your door with soup even if you didn't know her. Stella was devoted to her church and her community, and in 1980 she was gunned down at an ATM on Broadway. She was getting cash to buy ribbons for a Polish gymnastics team that was coming through Cleveland. (They later were the honor guard at her funeral.) After her death there was some question about Stella's true gender, which was no secret and no concern to the people who knew her. But keep in mind that she won a gold medal in the Olympics, and some people questioned whether she had done so legally. In its story about the controversy, WEWS ran the headline: "Coming up. Was Stella a fella?" There were so many angry calls that the writer never made it to the end of the newscast. He was fired and escorted from the building.

Even in the mid-1970s the stations weren't sure how much news the viewer wanted . . . or could take. Cleveland had morning and afternoon newspapers, and radio news was usually there at the top of every hour. Dick Lobo found that out the hard way when he became news director at WKYC-TV in 1973. He had serious credentials. Assignment editor at WNBC in New York, he jumped at the chance to head the newsroom in Cleveland. He also had major hurdles. Channel 3 was dead last and making no progress against WEWS and WJW, which had smaller staffs. Morale at Channel 3 was horrible. Plus, he had to deal with a new news set that drew immediate reaction from the viewers, and it was far from good. Some said it looked like a game-show set, but even more likened it to a bowling alley. The reaction was so negative that NBC brass in New York okayed a new (and expensive) set less than two months later. Lobo also introduced a ninety-minute news show that turned out to be very expensive with all the additional personnel. On top of that, Cleveland had plenty of slow news days, and there wasn't enough content to fill an hour and a half. There was another problem. Lobo found the worst enemy of Cleveland turned out to be Clevelanders!

Lobo told Bill Hickey at the *Plain Dealer*, "When I was offered this job, I was apprehensive about making such a move. I expected the very worst of all possible living situations. In a short time, however, I learned the city was the victim of a bum rap nationwide." He went on to say, "The worst thing about Cleveland is that the people who live here continually disparage the city. They're their own worst enemies, and if they don't soon realize that, there will be no hope for Cleveland. Some super jock or rock star will come here for two days and, when he can't find the kind of action he wants, will blast the city, terming it a graveyard or something equivalent. Clevelanders let that bother them to the point where they come to believe it themselves." He added, "This lack of self-confidence has hurt this city to no end. I know it has hurt me personally because I offered jobs to two top reporters, who could have helped Channel 3 news greatly. Both men turned me down, saying that there was simply no way they could live in Cleveland." Eventually it got to Lobo as well, and he left for an NBC gig in Denver just three years after his arrival at WKYC.

There are lots of practical jokes, but there's one that became a legend. Frankly, it never should have gotten as far as it did. Dan Coughlin, who tells the story best, calls it the "Gag of the Decade." It happened in May 1975. Mark Koontz was at WEWS and was told to do a live weather shot for the six o'clock news from the Party in the Park. Those were pretty much excuses for people to come out and drink beer in the streets of downtown Cleveland. He also had to do a story for the eleven o'clock show, so he took off right after he did the 6. Koontz got back to the station by 9 p.m. and was told he would have to fill in for Don Webster. He got right to work and sat down at Dave Patterson's desk. Patterson was anchoring with John Hambrick, who had his eye on a job in Los Angeles. They were just standing around the newsroom, when all of a sudden one of the film editors runs into the room screaming, "Mertens shot Polk!" Don Mertens was the head film editor, and Tom Polk was an assistant. In comes Mertens with a real .38 revolver! He puts the gun to Hambrick's head and pulls the trigger. Hambrick grabs his head, blood spurts out, and people are screaming and running out of the room. Mertens turns around and glares at Koontz. "You're next!" He aimed at Koontz, who jumped under the desk . . . right next to Hambrick, who's got blood all over his head. Not only that, there's blood all over Koontz, and he faints dead away. The place breaks out in laughter! The bullets were blanks, the blood was catsup, and they're waking Koontz up with smelling salts. They keep reassuring him, "Everything's okay. It was a joke!" This is where it gets even weirder. As the joke was happening, one of the Action Cam operators was on the phone with his cousin, a dispatcher at the Central Police Station. He didn't know what was happening and told the cops a gunman was loose in the Channel 5 building. A bunch of people are helping Koontz to the cafeteria, and police are banging on the door with their guns to let them in. It gets worse! News editors listen to police radios and Channels 3 and 8 sent film crews and reporters to WEWS. Word got out that it was a joke and everyone had a big laugh . . . except the cops. They made it clear that emotions run high and people could have been hurt. Even though the story never made it to air, newsrooms talk, and it was all over the country within a few days. That was not good news for John Hambrick, who thought it might hurt his chances on the west coast. As it turned out, it did not.

That's not to say there weren't some loose cannons in local newsrooms. Channel 3 once had a general manager named Neal Van Ells. He came to Cleveland after being profiled in a tabloid magazine called *On the QT* for allegedly breaking the jaw of his then-wife, singer Phyllis McGuire of the McGuire Sisters. Then he slugged a cameraman who questioned him about the incident. The case was reportedly settled for $3,500.

A lot more people smoked back then, and it was common to see reporters and even anchors lighting up on the air. Part of it was pressure, and some people couldn't handle it. That might have been the case with Murray Stewart. He had a big career before he made it to Cleveland. Network radio and TV, and even some work in movies. But there were demons, and he handled them the only way he could. Stewart came to Cleveland to anchor WJW's news. In August 1976 he came to work but called his partner Jim Finerty to say he couldn't do the noon newscast because he didn't feel well. Before he left he typed out the noon format with a note to Finerty that said, "See you later." He checked in to the Beachwood Holiday Inn, where he downed two bottles of Nembutal. A maintenance man found his body a few hours later. There was a note, but the family didn't reveal the contents. Stewart did have severe heart disease, but it might have been depression over the death of his four-year-old son sixteen years earlier that put him over the edge.

It can be dangerous work, too, and nobody knows that better than Del Donahoo. WKYC sent him out to the Midway Mall in Elyria in October 1976 for a feature on Dale Chivonic's "Lovable Lions." As it turns out, one was not so lovable. The act used volunteers as lion tamers. There were about three hundred people there watching as Del and Chivonic rode around a big cage on a lion. As Del was getting off, the lion rolled over and started to bite him! Del thought he was just playing until he saw blood and screamed for help. Chivonic beat the lion with a pole until he let Del loose, and he was rushed to Elyria Memorial Hospital. He walked out with forty-eight stitches and deep scar for a souvenir. Not to waste any tape, WKYC played part of it on their newscast, but it was a lot worse than what we saw on the screen.

News can be frustrating, especially if you consider yourself a journalist. The movie *Network* came out in 1976 and in many ways predicted trends we see today. Anchor Howard Beele became a superstar when he told viewers to go to their windows and scream, "I'M AS MAD AS HELL, AND I'M NOT GOING TO TAKE IT ANYMORE!" Dave Patterson didn't go that far, but his comments raised some eyebrows. The *Wall Street Journal* decided to run a story about all the Cleveland stations, and WEWS was riding high

Along with his reporting duties, Bill Jacocks was an accomplished singer and songwriter. His song "You Are the One" got a fair amount of airplay when it was released in the late 1970s. *Cleveland Press, author's collection*

in the ratings. The *WSJ* didn't hold back. It said news coverage was superficial and "few, if any stories (except for the weather report) are done in depth." Surprisingly, Patterson agreed. He said, "The only reason they call the show I'm on 'news' is that the title of it is *Eyewitness News*. It's really an entertainment program. and what they want of me is to be a literate buffoon." That won him a trip to the corporate woodshed. He had some 'splaining to do!

Then there's the case of former U.S. Marine Cory Moore. In March 1977 he walked into Warrensville Heights City Hall and took the police chief and a secretary hostage. Moore said he was concerned about the way blacks were treated and demanded "all white Americans leave the planet." Not only that, he wanted to speak directly with then-president Jimmy Carter. The feds and police departments from other cities rushed in to help and cordoned off several blocks around the city. Thankfully, cooler heads prevailed because sharpshooters across the street had a clear shot at Moore when he walked past windows in the rear of city hall, and one officer said he was ready to take his head off! They wanted to talk it through, but Moore kept hanging up the phone. Bill Jacocks was a pioneer black journalist at WEWS, and federal agents asked him to help. This put Bill into a delicate position because news reporters don't cross the line to become newsmakers. They have to be impartial, but lives were at stake here, and Bill ran out to the scene. He told the *Plain Dealer*, "It's true that I could have refused to take part of this situation; the police did not commandeer my services, but they did point out that my contributions might possibly save three lives. I decided it was something that I had to do, no matter the philosophical questions involved." That helped ease the tension, but it was far from over.

The Warrensville Heights police had a conversation and Bill called in Arnold Pinkney, who was president of the Cleveland school board and very prominent in the African American community. Moore was a fan of Pinkney and even voted for him when he ran for mayor. They spoke on the phone for about a half an hour, and Pinkey told the *Cleveland Press*, "He talked about blacks going hungry, about discrimination against black people and about black people unable to get jobs. As a black man I could sympathize with him. I told him this was not the way to protest. He wasn't militant or angry. This was just his way of doing it." Now everyone had to find a way to undo it.

They kept the lines open, and Pinkney told Moore the world was watching him. It was time to come out, especially for the sake of his family. "I know they love me," Moore said. "I don't want to hurt anybody. As soon as I talk to the President, the captain and I will walk out of here." By this time, media was everywhere—along with SWAT teams, who pulled back when Moore started to get nervous. This went on for another twelve hours. Police sent in food and drinks, but Moore stood his ground. Word came down that White House press secretary Jody Powell was aware of the situation and had even put in a request to President Carter. The White

House said a phone call could happen, but only if Moore released a hostage. Moore didn't want to hear it and kept hanging up on Pinkney. By the second day he had calmed down a bit and asked Pinkney to send in some food, orange juice for him and a steak dinner for the captain. Moore made it clear that he didn't have anything against the hostages personally. He liked the captain and said they had become friends, but no phone call and the standoff would continue. The White House blinked first. An agreement was made to mention the standoff, free the hostage and surrender, and Moore would get his call.

It happened on the morning of March 9. Carter acknowledged the standoff in a nationally televised press conference, telling a Scripps-Howard reporter, "The request was made to me to talk to Mr. Moore as a pre-condition for the release of the police officer. I understand the police officer is to be released after this news conference . . . I hope he will be released and if he is released, I will talk to Mr. Moore." Everyone lived up to his word. That afternoon a call came into the Warrensville Heights detective bureau. Reporters were kept away from the building, but the two did talk. Carter reportedly wished Moore luck, adding he realized racial discrimination was still prevalent in America. Moore hung up the phone, put down his gun, and was taken to the Cuyahoga County Grand Jury to face kidnapping charges. This set a dangerous precedent, as there was a lot of anger expressed in the way it was handled. Don Robertson at the *Cleveland Press* called the coverage a "media ripoff . . . . Television still has to learn how and when to use that sort of technology." WKYC's Neal Van Ells also went on the air to protest the way the siege was covered. It's anyone's guess whether he would have felt that way if Bill Jacocks had been working for his station, Channel 3.

Not every newsroom pursued this kind of journalism. In the days before the ten o'clock news WUAB had a weekly newscast that was pretty much a community bulletin board. It was just a couple of still photos and some upcoming events. The show was taped and ran late on Sunday nights, and it was anchored by Marty Sullivan.

Marty would tape his "Super Host" show, wipe the makeup off, and put on a dress shirt, tie, and jacket . . . but that was it. He just wore them over the blue long johns he used for the Super Host costume. If you had the same view as the crew you'd have seen him sitting behind the desk without pants! Years before that the crew at Channel 3 would be amazed at how calm and professional Jim Graner was even with technical glitches and movement all around him. Late on a Friday night when no one else was at the KYW building, a cameraman ran over to the Roxy Theater and paid a stripper to stop over between shows. During the eleven o'clock cast the anchors introduced Graner, and the stripper walked to the side of the camera and dropped her trench coat. That's all she was wearing! Graner didn't flinch. He gave his sports report and ran down all the scores from that night's high school football games. He just forgot to give the names of the teams! Just the numbers.

Then there were the two WEWS reporters who posed as hookers to get a story . . . and were stopped and questioned by police for suspicion of prostitution! It happened in the summer of 1977. Marge Banks and Tappy Phillips at Channel 5 wanted to see how effective Cleveland Police were at busting prostitutes. Turned out even they were surprised. Two cops spotted the two women talking to the drivers of cars "looking for a good time" near the WEWS station at East 30th and Euclid. When the two moved over to Prospect Avenue, police followed. The reporters had been investigating for about ten minutes when the boys in blue swooped in, in their unmarked car, and started asking questions. Marge and Tappy tried to explain what they were doing, but the police weren't buying it. Luckily, the videographer who was filming them was set up on the roof of a nearby building and saw what was happening. Calls were made and the reporters were allowed to go on their way, but not before a good finger-wagging by the police. They pointed out that when undercover police worked as decoys, they always had armed patrolmen to back them up.

From *Barn Dance* to *Upbeat*

Music Television Long Before MTV

CLEVELAND WAS A MUSIC town long before the Rock and Roll Hall of Fame. People in Northeast Ohio bought more records and books than anywhere else in the country, so it seemed natural that TV would "jump on the bandwagon." You have to remember that segregation was the norm back in the late '40s, so you weren't going to see much rhythm and blues. But Cleveland was known for two very popular forms of music, and TV was all over them: polkas and "hillbilly music." You had the *Barn Dance, Saturday Night Jamboree, Polka Time, Polka Revue,* and the list went on. The problem was, that kind of music appealed to old fogies. WEWS decided to go after teenagers with a record-hop show hosted by Bob Dale. It also had no budget! After Bob introduced a record, the camera panned down to a revolving turntable. When the song was over, it went back to him. They brought kids in to dance to the music, but every now and then one of them would bump into the record player and knock off the tone arm. The station brought that show to an end after a few weeks.

By 1950 Alan Freed had made his way to Cleveland, but it was for a TV gig. He left Akron's WAKR in hope of getting more money at WJW. Freed had a part-time job tending bar at a hotel in Kent to make ends meet, and the long hours were wearing him down. But he also had a noncompete clause in his contract at WAKR that stopped him from working at another radio station until that agreement ran out. Freed took a job at WXEL. TV didn't pay very well back then, but he had a family, and he could tread water and serve drinks until he could make the move to WJW.

By 1955 Bill Randle was a radio legend on WERE. He had an

ego as big as the Terminal Tower, and he could back up every word of it. Betty Cope gave Bill a chance for a late-night Sunday show on WEWS. There was no shortage of guests. A lot of big-name entertainers wanted to get on Bill's good side by performing on his show. Billy Eckstine, Spike Jones, and Sammy Watkins could have played high-paying gigs, but when Bill called you didn't have much choice. He could make them or break them. The show never really took off. At that hour most kids were in bed listening to the radio hidden under their pillow, and Bill didn't look right on TV. He had sensitive skin and wouldn't wear makeup because he would break out in acne. Even so, national TV took note of Bill Randle. He also had a show on WCBS radio in New York on weekends and was mentioned in an episode of *The Honeymooners*. Plus, he introduced Elvis Presley to a national audience on the Dorsey Brothers' show. That was a major appearance. Acne or not, they plastered on the makeup with a trowel.

Bill wasn't an easy guy to work with. He griped a lot, and if you didn't bow in reverence, you ended up on his list. That list had to be the size of the Manhattan phone book! He especially didn't like one of his coworkers at WERE, Phil McLean. Phil had a deep voice that started in the basement, and people loved him because of his easy-going style. He didn't have a huge ego, and in many ways he was the Bizarro Randle. He even put out a record slamming Randle, called "Big Mouth Bill." It had to sting when Channel 5 announced that Phil would co-host its *Bandstand* show. If anything, it lit a fire under Bill. He pulled every string he could to get bigger stars for his Sunday night show. Fess Parker dropped by to plug his Davy Crockett show and sing his new record "Ringle Rangle" (without the coonskin cap!). Tab Hunter did the show, too, but his label insisted the only way he could do his new record was if he lip-synched it. Tab looked great, but he really couldn't sing. It didn't really matter. Channel 5 was looking to replace Randle. Word got around, and resumes started pouring in. One of them came from Philadelphia. That city had its own *Bandstand*, hosted by one of the city's most popular disc jockeys. It was a hit show, on every day, easy money, and the host wasn't going anywhere. Then there was a DUI charge (when the station was doing a series on drunk driving) and a morals charge for soliciting a prostitute. The jock who applied at WEWS got the job in Philly, but until that time, Dick Clark . . . yes, that Dick Clark . . . was ready to move to Cleveland. The fact is that Bill Randle may have aired too much of the music he liked rather than what the kids wanted. By 1957 Alan Freed had moved on to New York after his notoriety in Cleveland and got a nationally syndicated show on ABC. It was called the *Rock and Roll Revue,* and while Bill Randle had guests like Chico Hamilton and Teresa Brewer, Freed gave an audience to Chuck Berry, Ricky Nelson, and Buddy Holly.

Channel 5 wasn't giving up on local talent. In 1958 the station gave Bill "Smoochie" Gordon a try. His ratings were huge on WHK-AM, but Bill had two issues: He rambled on and rarely finished a sentence. "Hey, did you see that . . . I can't believe . . . you know when you gotta . . . I was amazed." The only thing he seemed to say with any clarity was, "Stay smoochie, you rascal you!" which was obviously his catch phrase. Second, he never shut up! Bill was a born entertainer, but as Groucho Marx would have said, he was "vaccinated with a phonograph needle." The producers had a hard time reining him in. When *Bill Gordon's Saturday Night Party* premiered that summer, he went on for twenty-eight minutes straight before he introduced the band. The floor director was pulling his hair out, and the sales manager started waving goodbye to commercials they could never make up. People liked Bill, but the show didn't last long. Why buy time on a show that can't get in your commercials?

There was another problem. Bill didn't like rock and roll. He had a great reputation in radio, although WHK did give him his walking papers for talking over records. He was one of fifteen disc jockeys chosen to fill in for Dick Clark on *American Bandstand* when he took a three-week vacation. Bill flew to Philadelphia, and it turned into a train wreck. His jokes fell flat. "Hello, I'm Dick Clark for a day! What a financial pleasure it is to be here!" Silence, and it spiraled down from there. He spent most of the time saying

Bill Gordon was a born talker on radio and TV. The problem was, there were times when he didn't know when to stop talking. *Cleveland Press, author's collection*

hello to folks back in Cleveland and plugging WEWS. It turned into a long day on both sides of the camera. Bill was not asked to return.

It wasn't all rock and roll. Every station also had musicians performing all day in the background of the live shows. Folks like Crandall Hendershott, Blanche Albritton, and Joe Howard would sit down at the keyboard for eight hours and do live intros, fill music, and even theme songs, then punch out and go home. They really got a workout backing Paige Palmer and *Romper Room* host Miss Barbara because those women depended heavily on background music. Crandall said he played behind the shows as if they were silent movies. Howard backed up everyone from Elvis Presley to Duke Ellington, plus he had gigs at the Poodle Lounge, the Theatrical, and other clubs along with his TV job.

Grant Wilson led a busy day at WJW, playing for the station's

If it's Sunday, it's *Polka Varieties*. Host Paul Wilcox celebrates his anniversary on the show with producer Herman Spero, Al Herrick, and polka legend Frank Yankovic. *Cleveland Press, author's collection*

Kids Bits in the morning, various assignments during the day, and then finishing up at the Encore Room nightclub in Shaker Heights. His instrument of choice was the celestina, a portable keyboard. Wilson had quite a resumé playing vaudeville shows at the Palace Theatre and on TV with Gloria Gale and Alan Freed, and on the *King Jack* kids' show. But what do you think was the most popular music on TV at that time? What else? Polkas! Because of the city's heavy ethnic mix, polkas became a favorite form of programming, and as early as 1954 WEWS had a show hosted by Kenny Bass. But there was another announcer standing in the wings that would become synonymous with the city's polka community.

WEWS saw the potential in a young sportscaster from WGAR named Paul Wilcox, who took a long and dangerous road to his career in television. He was born in Sylvania and worked at

WHRV-AM/Ann Arbor after he earned his degree at the University of Michigan.

Paul, a World War II veteran who flew twenty-three missions in the Pacific with the 20th Air Force, won the Distinguished Flying Cross and Air Medal for his efforts. He joined the staff at WGAR in February 1950 and settled in for what he hoped would be a long and prosperous career in broadcasting. Then in 1951, Paul was recalled for reserve duty and shipped out to Korea that October. On Dec. 30, 1952, Lieutenant Wilcox was flying as a bombardier aboard a B-29 near Chonchou in North Korea when an enemy MIG brought down his plane in a hail of gunfire. The twenty-seven–year-old was listed as missing in action.

As it turns out, Paul parachuted to safety but was quickly taken prisoner. He would later recall, "It was like a freak show. In every village they marched me through I was put on display. There were no friendly faces." The Koreans took all his personal property, including his wedding ring. Eventually, he was introduced to Chinese military personnel, who got into a dispute with the Koreans over his custody and that of another prisoner. Paul went with the Chinese, while the other prisoner remained with the Korean soldiers.

When he arrived at a POW detention center, Paul was placed in solitary confinement for four months and also faced intense interrogation. His captors wanted him to confess to engaging in germ warfare and warned him, "You're a war criminal and you'll be treated as one!" But when they learned of his background in radio, they shifted to quizzing him about American slang they could use in propaganda broadcasts to U.N. troops on the line. Paul was clever enough to give terms that sounded legitimate but would make the broadcasts sound ludicrous to anyone hearing the shows.

Paul was repatriated back to the United States on August 31, 1953, and received a hero's welcome when he arrived at Cleveland Airport that September, an event that prompted great hometown media interest. Paul started doing sports part-time at WEWS, and *Press* writer Stan Anderson even suggested he had the looks for a

Country music had an early foothold on Cleveland TV, even when people thought it was just "cowboy songs." Disc jockey Tommy Edwards is seen on WEWS' *Landmark Jubilee* with Cleveland housewife Dottie West, who would have a long and successful yet tragic career in music. *Cleveland Press Collection, Cleveland State University Archives*

career on the big screen. Paul never made that move but remained one of the area's most respected and admired TV performers. In 1958 Paul Wilcox became the face and voice of *Polka Varieties*.

In 1959 Channel 5 started syndicating country music with the *Landmark Jamboree* show. Tommy Edwards was the host, and he had a keen ear for country. He played it on his show on WERE and, truth be told, he introduced Elvis on stage before Bill Randle. Tommy staged "Hillbilly Hayride" shows at the Circle Theater at East 105th, and Elvis played there the night before the Brooklyn High School show. Another Tommy Edwards discovery was Dottie West, a Cleveland housewife who would end up in the Country Music Hall of Fame. Dottie had a tragic life and would often say her best days were in Cleveland. Gene Carroll also had his *Giant Tiger Amateur Hour*, which was really a way to mostly showcase people who came through his talent school. It later became the *Gene Carroll Show,* and some even went on to stardom. Andrea Carroll had a hit with "Please Don't Talk to the Lifeguard," and Chrissie Hynde of the Pretenders and Bobby Womack would be inducted into the Rock and Roll Hall of Fame. Ben Orr of the Cars got a shot on the program, as well. Ben was with the Grasshoppers and used the name "Benny Eleven Letters" because no one could pronounce Orzechowski. He would also play a major role in Cleveland's best-known music show.

It was early 1964. The Beatles had been on *The Ed Sullivan Show,* and we were starting to loosen up a bit after the Kennedy assassination the year before. Pop culture had kicked into high gear. Think back to that time: the Civil Rights movement, the Cold War, the space race, Viet Nam . . . . The only thing kids cared about in Cleveland were Ghoulardi and the Beatles.

There were a lot of big names coming through Cleveland for shows in clubs such as Otto's Grotto and Leo's Casino. They did good business, but it didn't hurt to get the word out, and TV was the place to do it. Herman Spero had produced a number of shows at WEWS and, together with a director named Al Herrick and Dick Blake (the dance teacher), they came up with *The Big 5 Show.* They could get acts to come in for free to lip synch their songs and plug their concerts. Win-win for everyone, and at the right price! They got a couple of WHK disc jockeys, Johnny Walters and Ron Britain, to host the first shows, and it worked like a charm. Cleveland finally had a cool music show! The only snag was that the jocks from WHK were obviously radio guys and didn't look comfortable on TV. Enter Don Webster.

He came down from CHCH-TV in Toronto to host a game show at Channel 5, *Quick as a Wink.* It was supposed to compete with the last half hour of *The Mike Douglas Show,* but the ratings showed it wasn't even close. Don had lots of TV experience and even did news. They needed a place for him, and he got assigned to *The Big 5 Show.* It started to take off, and with all the star power coming through Cleveland it wasn't hard to syndicate. Stations across the

Upbeat was syndicated across the country and attracted some of the biggest stars of the day. Here Davy Jones (left) and Mickey Dolenz (right) of The Monkees chat with WEWS host Don Webster. *Cleveland Press Collection, Cleveland State University Archives*

country started signing up, especially after it went to color. But *The Big 5 Show* didn't mean anything to people in Poughkeepsie unless it aired at five o'clock, so they changed the name to the more generic *Upbeat*.

Even the syndication was primitive. They used big reels of two-inch video tape, which they would "bicycle" across the country. When one station aired the show it would be sent to another city, then another and another. Since the tape was so expensive (about a dollar a second) they would reuse the reels when they got back to Channel 5 and send them back on the road. That meant a lot of wear. That's also a big reason we don't see the show repackaged for home video. On top of that, the artists would lip synch. If they performed live, that performance belonged to the show's producers. But they didn't own the performance on record. If the Fifth Dimension lip-synched "Up, Up and Away," the producers owned the video of the dance they did on set and nothing else.

Needless to say, the other stations saw the ratings and scrambled to put on their own shows. WKYC had Jerry G. Bishop from its radio side with *Jerry G and Company*, but that came to an end when he landed a gig in Chicago. Others just depended on syndicated shows.

Some of the biggest names came to *Upbeat*. Although they didn't perform, the Beatles were interviewed on film just after their 1964 Cleveland press conference. It ran the gamut from cheesy acts like Bobby Sherman and the 1910 Fruitgum Company to more "credible" acts like Sly and the Family Stone, Simon and Garfunkel, and the Yardbirds with Jimmy Page. There's one performance that stands out to this day.

In December 1967, Otis Redding and the Bar-Kays were booked to play Leo's Casino. Redding was on the verge of superstardom. He got rave reviews at the Monterey Pop Festival a few months before, and he was selling out clubs after that. He was scheduled to tape an *Upbeat* show and came in late saying there were problems with his private plane. Redding really wanted to do *Upbeat* because one of his best friends, Johnny Daye of Pittsburgh, had been booked for the same show. He sang "Respect" and "Try a Little Tenderness," then closed the show with Mitch Ryder singing Eddie Floyd's "Knock on Wood." That night he played Leo's and died a few hours later in a plane crash with four members of his band in Lake Monona, Wisconsin. Redding was only twenty-six. The *Upbeat* show aired a couple of days after he died, and his biggest hit "(Sittin' on) The Dock of the Bay" came out the next month. *Upbeat* lasted until 1971. The ad money was drying up, and some of the key markets dropped the show. It was time to pull the plug.

"My Dog's Name Is Barnaby"

Linn Sheldon and the Birth of Children's Television

BACK IN THE 1940s Cleveland's nightclub scene ranked right up there with Chicago, Los Angeles, and even New York. Those were the days when there were two downtowns, at Public Square and at 105th and Euclid, and fancy supper clubs, theaters, and speakeasies lined the streets. The Crystal Ballroom, Cotton Club, Chin's . . . the list went on. Stars would play two weeks at Playhouse Square and head down the street to 105th for another week after that. If you made it to Cleveland, you made it to the big time, and if you got booked at Herman Pirchner's Alpine Village, you were on top of the world. Herman was a real character and people came to see him perform as much as they did the headliners. He dressed like an Alpine yodeler, and you always knew when Herman was in the house. He had a booming voice, and he could balance more than fifty heavy steins of beer on a tray, then slide on his knees down to the end of a table without spilling a drop. That was the bit that got him featured in the *March of Time* newsreels and *Ripley's Believe it or Not*. There was something about TV that intrigued him. He could provide the content and get plenty of free advertising for his club, and he knew just the guy to pull it off.

Linn Sheldon didn't want to go in to television. Well, let's just say he didn't see a need to. He was already one of Cleveland's biggest (and highest paid) actors. Linn couldn't walk down the street without someone rushing up to shake his hand. He'd even done films with Spencer Tracy and Hedy Lamarr. Plus, Linn got a lot of work at the Alpine Village, performing with some of the biggest stars on the circuit. "Lonesome George" Gobel, Dean Martin and

"Introduce yourself to me. My name is Barnaby!" Linn
Sheldon played a lot of roles but will always be known for the
kids' show that made him a legend. *Cleveland Press, author's collection*

Jerry Lewis, Count Basie. Linn knew them all, and they loved
working with him. Who would remember him from television? He
didn't even know anyone who had a television. Herman Pirchner
thought otherwise. He would bring in his headline acts on a weekly
basis, and Linn would be the host. That's how Linn Sheldon found
himself at the door of WEWS.

Herman's idea was a good one, but it didn't fill up a lot of time,
and TV is like a hungry elephant. Those were the days when you
couldn't publish a TV listing because no one at the station knew
what would be on the air that night. Linn recalled, "You could walk
into the boss's office and say 'I can spin plates.' 'Can you do it for a
half an hour?' 'Sure!' 'You got a show. You're on in five minutes.'" It

was only on for a few hours a night, but the station had a hard time filling out the schedule. Plus, anything could and did happen with live TV. The stage lights could be brutal, and WEWS didn't have air conditioning. During the summer they kept every door open just to keep the air moving, but they found out the hard way that it wasn't such a good idea. Linn was doing a live show one evening when a guy walked in off the street and went right up to him. "Hey, pal, where's the toilet?" Linn didn't blink and sent him down the hall. A couple of minutes later Linn was still on the air and the same guy came by to say, "Thanks a lot, but you might want to get more soap in there." It didn't faze Linn Sheldon. He just pointed to the red light on the camera, the guy's eyes popped out of his head, and they cut to a commercial.

That happened more than once. Linn had a live fifteen-minute variety show sponsored by Rodgers Jewelers. One of the guys at Rodgers wanted to see his girlfriend on TV, so Linn hired her as the "talent," the spokesperson. Problem was, she was terrified of public speaking and didn't want to be on camera. "Just go out there and do the commercial!" They set the commercial up with a black velvet cloth draped over a desk and a display of diamond rings. It didn't go well. The woman was having problems showing the jewelry and started to cry. All of a sudden she blurted out, "I told that son-of-a-bitch I didn't want to do this!" Then she threw the diamonds at the camera and stormed off the set. Linn just introduced the next act.

Cleveland got nailed with a blizzard on Thanksgiving weekend in 1950. It hit like a cyclone with heavy snow and high winds, and it paralyzed the city. Linn and his old friend Bob Dale were at the station when the snow started to fall and they got the call to stay put. Linn remembered it well. "We got a call to stay there and keep updating the audience every now and then. We were across from the Hotel Manger [the old Allerton hotel], and the management said Bob and I should get rooms and take our meals there until the emergency was over. Luckily, a girls' drill team from Texas was there as well, and Bob and I would excuse ourselves from enter-

Barnaby's fans were legion, and they were not happy when his show was pre-empted by a World Series game in 1958. *Cleveland Press, author's collection*

taining them in the lounge to go across the street, give an update, and head right back!"

Linn was born to do TV. Show biz was in his blood, and it wasn't long before Linn and his wife Vivian had their own program twice a week. *The Sheldons* was almost like a modern- day reality show, and he found inspiration anywhere, any time. Lying in bed with an idea for a sketch, Linn would jump out of the sack and have Vivian shine a spotlight on him for a "television effect." The show had music, interviews, and comedy . . . although some of that comedy was unintentional. It was one of Linn's favorite stories.

"The stage crew built these elaborate sets. On our first show, we decided to lip synch a duet to a song called 'Come Out, Come Out, My Little Kitten.' They had a set that looked like the front of a

house, and Vivian was on top of a ladder looking out the window. I
came around the corner doing my part of the song, and I looked up
and couldn't stop laughing. I had to keep my back to the camera.
When it was over, Vivian asked, 'What was that all about?' I pointed
to above the window. Someone had painted 'Cathouse' because of
the song. They sure didn't know the meaning of cathouse."

Vivian also helped write and produce Linn's *Big Wheels* show.
Sponsored by the *Cleveland Press*, it offered kids who wrote to
the program a chance to work in the occupation they hoped for
as an adult. Some of them became nurses, financiers, even a jet
pilot, after they saw how those jobs worked on *Big Wheels*. One kid
wanted to see what it was like to be a millionaire, so they filmed
him in a bank vault surrounded by a million dollars. When it was
over the kid walked out . . . and the cops frisked Linn.

Most of the old-time entertainers would tell you: "Don't work
with kids or dogs. They steal the show." Not Linn Sheldon. He
brought out the best in kids, and vice versa. His first children's
show, *Uncle Leslie,* was about a hobo clown. It was sponsored by
Tip-Top bread, and Uncle Leslie sold a lot of Tip-Top bread, snack
cakes, and everything else that came out of their ovens. WEWS had
a goldmine, but Linn wasn't seeing the gold. He turned in his resignation to do "Bob and Ray"-type spots for the Browns and Weide-
mann Beer with Jim Doney. But Channel 5 had had a back-up
plan in place for some time. In fact, Linn himself recommended
to Betty Cope that she use "the new kid, the staff announcer with
the deep voice." His name was Ron Penfound, and for a short time
they worked together at Channel 5. More on that to come.

Linn was able to bring in extra money hosting movies, and he
would invent a new character for each film. Gunfighters, old ladies,
pirates . . . he did them all. He was the king of improv, and those
characters would jump out of the screen. Word got around that
KYW was looking for someone to host the package of Popeye cartoons they bought, and after a couple of phone calls Linn turned
in his notice. There was more money, too, but Linn had to come
up with a character. In September 1957, Linn put on some wax

ears and a straw boater and was ready to conquer the world. One problem: Just as the cameras were ready to roll he realized the character didn't have a name! A stagehand said, "My dog's name is Barnaby." The legend was born.

Barnaby and *Popeye Theater* was never meant to be a kids' show. Parents loved him, too. It was pure entertainment, and the ratings shot through the roof. But even in 1957 there were folks who didn't have TVs or didn't know about Barnaby. The show aired in late afternoon when lots of folks were still at work. That became evident when Linn went to buy mortician's wax to form his ears. He was at the store every couple of weeks, and the owner thought Linn was a funeral director. He said, "You must have one hell of a business!" Linn replied, "Oh, I use it on myself." He saw the owner do a double-take, and Linn went on his way. Another time, Linn was going to shoot some footage at Edgewater Park in Lakewood. It was a brutally hot day, and he was in full makeup, including mascara. While he waited for the cameraman he scouted out some spots to shoot in the woods. The heat started to get to him, and Linn walked out from the trees to look for the camera. He came upon a caretaker cutting grass on a riding mower. Keep in mind the heavy makeup and pixie ears. "Hey buddy! I'm looking for somebody." Lakewood had a reputation even then. The caretaker got a load of Barnaby and floored the mower in a beeline toward the street. Linn could only think, "Wow! I didn't know those things could go that fast."

Hiring Linn Sheldon reaped huge rewards. Complaints started coming into KYW. Everyone loved Barnaby, but he was way too good at his job! For parents serving an early dinner, the combination of Barnaby and *The Mickey Mouse Club* was a one-two punch. Kids wolfed down their food to get back to the screen, and some moms even rescheduled dinner for a later hour. The cartoons were popular, but Linn was the draw, and he didn't just play Barnaby. He could play two or three different characters in one show!

When you have a marquee name like Barnaby, you look to make as much money as you can. Walt Disney cleaned up on mouse

Barnaby was a huge draw on and off the screen.
He's seen here hosting the Ringling Brothers circus
at the Coliseum in Richfield in the 1970s. *Cleveland
Press, author's collection*

ears and coonskin caps, and Mickey's novelty records took off
like a rocket. Let's see what Barnaby could do. On Thanksgiving
Day 1958, Cleveland heard for the very first time "Boofo Goes
Where Santa Goes," and stores couldn't keep it on the shelves. It
was released by Cosmic Records with the flip side "Rabbits Have
a Christmas," and radio and TV played it endlessly. There was a
near mob scene with fans crowding in to buy records at Higbee's,
and at every Barnaby appearance the stores would play it over and
over to the point where Linn said he grew to hate it! The public

thought otherwise. It became every bit as famous as Barnaby's theme song "A La Claire Fontaine (At the Clear Fountain)," and years later the *Wall Street Journal* reported it would be played at Christmas parties at the American Embassy in Moscow well into the 1990s. Even so, Linn made sure that was the end of Barnaby's recording career.

Keep in mind that this was live TV. It was like walking a tight-rope without a net, and on more than one occasion Linn had to think fast to avert disaster. One of the bits from the show was an invisible parrot named Long John, which was Linn throwing his voice. KYW had a contest for kids to draw Long John, and the winner would get a brand new bike. The manufacturer also wanted film of the winner getting his or her prize. Cameras rolled, and a six-year-old—let's call him Bobby—was live with Barnaby on the air. The conversation went like this:

"Well, Bobby, take a look at this great bike. It's got a headlight, a basket . . . what do you think?"

Bobby said, "Thanks, Barnaby! I need a bike. A [expletive] stole mine."

Bobby had dropped the N bomb.

Linn got a chill up his back.

"This is one terrific bike, Bobby. You've got streamers, a horn . . . "

"Maybe you didn't hear me, Barnaby. A [expletive] stole my other bike." Another N bomb.

Sweat poured out from underneath Barnaby's straw boater. He had to get this kid's mind off the bike. "Bobby, you did such a great job on that picture. Did your dad help you?"

"Nah," the boy said. "One of my mom's friends. He comes over and takes naps with my mom when my dad is at work."

At that point, the mother raced onto the set, grabbed Bobby by the hand, and headed for the door. Linn was left holding the handlebars and looking into the camera. "Let's see what Popeye is up to!" They filmed the giveaway off screen with another kid, and no one was the wiser.

Advertisers loved Barnaby, but they didn't always like what he said. Linn was never condescending to the audience. He wanted kids to be creative and use their imaginations and, above all, just enjoy being a kid. On a nice day, he might say, "Hey, I'll be here tomorrow. Why not go outside and enjoy the sunshine? You can read a book or play a game with some friends! Barnaby will always be here for you, but get out there and have a great time!" Even so, a lot of people wanted to put money into his show.

Back in 1961 there were only six McDonald's restaurants in Northeast Ohio, and they were failing fast. Average store sales had dipped to $220,000 that year, down from $256,000 in 1960. Their consultant, Nick Karos, thought TV might be the answer, and he came up with an idea for an advertising cooperative. The operators kicked in $7,000 apiece, or about 3 percent of their sales, to advertise on a local kids' show, and their first choice was Barnaby's. The ads started on a Thursday, and no one was ready for what happened next. Within a couple of days the restaurants were running out of food, giving McDonald's a new lease on life. In fact, author John Love points out in his book, *McDonald's: Behind the Arches* (Bantam, 1995), that the Greater Cleveland plan would be the model for all the other regional and national co-ops in the system, accounting for nearly all of McDonald's advertising revenue. They loved Barnaby! They even offered Linn his own franchise, but he turned them down. He was a TV guy, and he wasn't sure fast-food restaurants would make it.

Barnaby knew how to move product, but at least one time it was product without profit. The Wham-O Toy Company introduced hula hoops back in the late 1950s. They took off like wildfire! A local guy saw an opportunity and bought a semi full of them, knowing he could unload them if he could get a crowd, and Barnaby could draw a crowd! He paid Linn to plug Barnaby's appearance and the hula hoops at a local shopping center. Linn couldn't remember the shopping center, but he sure knew the outcome. He got up on a riser at the end of the truck and saw a sea of little heads, thousands of them, with an occasional mom or dad. The crowd went wild,

Linn Sheldon was one of the great improv actors to ever appear on Cleveland TV. Here, he picks up a couple of model planes to spin a tale off the top of his head about two pilots in a mid-air meeting. *Cleveland Press, author's collection*

and before Linn could say who to pay for a hoop, a hand shot up in the crowd. "Hey, Barnaby! It's my birthday!" Linn didn't blink. "Then you get a free one! Any other birthdays?" What were the odds? Turns out *everyone* in the crowd was celebrating a birthday! Linn handed out one after another until the truck was pretty much empty. When the smoke cleared, Linn walked past the guy who had hired him. He was sitting in the cab of the truck with his eyes and mouth wide open, staring at the ceiling. Shock and awe!

Channel 3, now with the call letters WKYC, knew it had a winner, but Linn thought the act was getting a little old. He even had some doubts about the whole format. He told Bill Barrett at the *Cleveland Press*, "The children have got to face reality. They've got to learn that they can't solve their problems by watching cartoons all the time. Someone has got to say to them, 'Kids, tomorrow you'll step out in that world, and it can be a pretty rough place.'" He called television a "babysitter" and said, "We can't live in a fantasy world all our lives." That raised eyebrows at the station and on the street.

Every now and then Linn would find himself in a unique situation that left a lasting impression. Air travel was nowhere near as common in the mid-1950s as it is today, so if you booked a flight, it was an event. When he told the story, Linn couldn't remember where he was traveling from, but he knew he was heading back to Cleveland. As he was being led to his seat, the stewardess mentioned that Linn would be seated next to a celebrity, Grandma Moses, the famous painter. She was already in her nineties and the last person you expected to see on an airplane. "Hello, Mother! How are you? My name is Linn." The flight took off, and they were having a nice chat when all of a sudden the plane started to shake violently! As stewardesses hurried down the aisles, the pilot got on the public address system to say they had hit "a little turbulence." They would also be sending around a complimentary drink cart, and not soon enough for some folks! The plane rocked back and forth, obviously in trouble. Grandma Moses grabbed Linn's arm, screaming, "Help me! Please help!" Linn said he threw off her hands and said, "Let go of me, you old bat!" and took a couple of bottles off the drink cart. "I'll just help myself." Following an emergency landing, the staff hustled Grandma off the plane. By the time Linn made it to the terminal, he saw Grandma in a bar with her second double.

Linn had a lot of friends in show business and kept in touch with most of them. He met a lot of them during his time at the Alpine Village, but some, like Ray Walston (*My Favorite Martian*), were from Cleveland and did theater with him. In 1967 Linn got an invitation to appear on *The Tonight Show*. Bob Newhart was a fan of Linn's and was subbing that week for Johnny Carson. Linn flew out to do the show and was surprised to find another former Clevelander, Joel Grey, on the same bill. They'd never been

Linn Sheldon as Barnaby, having a heart-to-heart discussion with Long John, "the world's only invisible parrot." *Cleveland Press, author's collection*

friends. Grey made a crack about Linn during the rehearsal, which Linn pretty much ignored. Grey might have been worried, and with good reason, that Linn would steal the show. Unfortunately, Cleveland didn't get to see that episode because an Indians game on the West Coast ran late.

Linn wanted to cut back on Barnaby and do a talk show. The

station fought the move, but Linn eventually got his chance and in August 1968, he signed on at WKBF, Channel 61. Problem was, he had created a monster! People still wanted Barnaby, so Linn's talk show days were numbered. He took some other jobs on the creative end before winding up his TV career in 1990, as Barnaby, at WUAB.

Linn once said, "I never cease to be amazed about Barnaby. I never expected it to go so long. I say there were three reasons for the success of Barnaby. First, the time was right. Second, the cartoons were new. And last, the period the city was in. Cleveland needed a good children's show. I think my background in the theater, nightclubs, and movies helped. And I have a sincere love for children. I'm one myself—just a tall child."

Author's note: Linn Sheldon probably never knew the wide-ranging impact he had on people.

A few years ago I asked Don Novello to do a video introduction for a broadcasters' event. You know him better as Father Guido Sarducci from *Saturday Night Live.* Don was visiting his family in Lorain, and we made plans to do the taping at Swingo's Restaurant in Lakewood. Linn and Laura Sheldon lived right next door, so we made plans to have dinner with them at Swingo's after the shoot. As Don walked into the restaurant, he grabbed my arm and blurted out, "Is that Linn Sheldon?!" He couldn't wait to meet him, and Linn didn't know who he was. You could tell how much he admired Linn by the way he followed every word. Mind you, Don Novello worked with some of the biggest names in show business, but he couldn't believe he was sitting with Linn Sheldon! Before he left, my wife Janice took a photo that stood out from the hundreds of famous folks who lined the walls there. To the day he closed, Jim Swingo was still getting questions about the photo of him, Linn, and Father Guido Sarducci. Linn liked Don, too. A few weeks later Don sent me one of his books, *The Laszlo Letters*, with a note saying how much he had enjoyed the time he had spent with us. He also sent a card naming me a cardinal in his church. Later that day I stopped over at Linn's condo, and he showed me the same book, but his card was different. Don named him the pope!

Linn and I usually had lunch every couple of weeks at a diner in Lakewood. We were there so often that the waitresses would ask, "Do you guys want menus or just the usual?" One day Linn said, "Yeah, the usual. By the way, what do I usually get?" She said, "Two eggs poached, corned beef hash, no potatoes or bread because you might eat them." We were obviously there a lot. In his last years Linn was moving a lot slower. As we sat down for lunch, I happened to notice a guy I had gone to high school with years before. He waved me over to say hello and, of course, to ask, "Is that Barnaby?" I turned to go back to the table and bumped into Linn, who couldn't wait to say hello to my friend and his companions. I'm pretty sure that for the rest of the day my former schoolmate wasn't talking about *me*.

Linn's health problems were starting to wear on him. During one of the last times we met for lunch, Linn stopped me before we went in the door and said, "Let me ask you something. I played a hundred roles. Why is it whenever people introduce me it's always Linn 'Barnaby' Sheldon? It was just one role! I'm sure they wouldn't say Charles 'Quasimodo' Laughton. I don't get it." It was also a bitter cold morning in January, and I was freezing. "Linn, it's nice to be remembered," and we walked in to take a seat. It was between breakfast and lunch, so hardly anyone was there. Thankfully! As we walked in, a guy turned around in his seat with his mouth and eyes wide open. Linn looked at me and said, "Here it comes!" The waitress put us at a table next to four Cleveland cops, and we weren't in those seats more than a minute before the guy walked over and grabbed Linn's hand to shake it. In a loud voice he started saying, "Well, hello, Barnaby. How you doing, Barnaby? Barnaby, do you come here often?" Linn forced a smile, but you could tell he wasn't happy. He said, "Thank you. It's so nice to be remembered. We're going to have some coffee now, but thanks again." The fan walked back to the counter and Linn shook his head. A few minutes later we order and get some coffee, and the guy is back. Linn has coffee in one hand and the guy is shaking the other, and he's just as loud as he was before. "You know, Barnaby, you used to have this invisible bird and blah, blah, blah . . ." When he was done, Linn put down his cup, looked at him, and said, "It's so nice that you remembered. Thank you again, but my friend and I have to discuss some things." As he walked away, Linn rolled his eyes. The waitress brought our plates and Linn took a forkful in his right hand. Guess who's back? The guy picks up Linn's left hand and starts shaking it, saying, "Hey, Barnaby, I used to watch you every day, and I remember how you would end your show." Linn gave a sarcastic smile and said, "Tell 'em Barnaby said hello." The guy said, "No. You would say, 'You can fool some of the people some of the time . . .'" At this point it was like watching a car wreck in slow motion. I won't repeat what Linn actually said, but I can assure you that Barnaby would have never used *those* particular words. As the fan's eyes bugged out of his head, he looked shell-shocked, and the cops at the next table all dropped their shoulders laughing. Linn ended with, "Now, if you don't mind, we'd like to eat our lunch!" The guy went back to his seat not knowing what had hit him.

We tend to define and remember TV people by what we see on the screen. As Linn pointed out, Barnaby was a character, one of many roles he played over a long career. But it was a role that became bigger than Linn himself, thanks to a new medium and a very receptive audience. Plus, he was one of those rare entertainers who could connect with an audience on every level, young and old, from every nationality. With Cleveland's ethnic diversity, that cut a very wide path.

Certain things stay with you. To this day, the baby boomers can still tell you how Barnaby ended every show. "If anybody calls, tell them Barnaby said hello. And tell them that I think that you are the nicest person in the whole world. Yes, you. Just you."

"If you want to talk to me you can come to Cleveland!"

Dorothy Fuldheim, Cleveland's Grande Dame of Television

SOME PEOPLE WOULD SAY Dorothy Fuldheim was an old crank. But she was our old crank, and that added to her legend.

She grew up poor in Milwaukee. In fact, her family was so poor that when her baby brother died he had to be buried in an orange crate because they couldn't afford a coffin. But Dorothy's father had come to the United States from Germany because it promised opportunity, and he never stopped working to give his family a better life. He would take Dorothy to courthouses to see how eloquently lawyers spoke, which might have led to her becoming a teacher. In college Dorothy became an actress and got really positive reviews. The social worker Jane Addams told her to take her stage work on the road to push social reform. Dorothy went on the lecture circuit and did a lot of homework and interviews for every speech. That's what led her to Germany in 1932.

Most people in the United States didn't want another war and turned their back on what Hitler was doing in Germany. Not Dorothy Fuldheim. She sailed to Europe, made her way to Germany, and found out that Adolf Hitler would be appearing at the same beer hall in Munich where he tried to take over the government in 1923. He failed then, but nine years after the putsch, Hitler was seen in a new light. When Hitler walked into the beer hall, Dorothy saw an opportunity and took it. Years later she remembered, "I saw him walk into this hall where some diplomats were gathering, and I just walked up to him and started talking in German. We chatted about some very innocent things for about fifteen minutes. He didn't know I was Jewish." And what do you think they talked about? The beer hall was a public space, and they were holding a flower show. Dorothy Fuldheim talked to Hitler about flowers . . . but he said she sure knew a lot about flowers!

Dorothy started writing, and it wasn't long before she took a shot at radio. She got a lot of attention for her commentaries and style and eventually made her way to Cleveland's WJW-AM, and soon after WEWS-FM. It's now WDOK. The station was going to branch out to TV, too, and that could mean some extra money. In 1947 Dorothy Fuldheim was fifty-four years old and made her debut on the new Channel 5. They gave her a tryout for a fifteen-minute commentary after the news, one that was supposed to last thirteen weeks. That segment ran for seventeen years.

There weren't many women in broadcasting. Dorothy was a novelty, especially at her age, and that helped open doors. Sometimes she kicked the doors open. In 1950, when the Duke and Duchess of Windsor came to Cleveland, Dorothy marched over to the Hotel Statler with a couple of cameramen. She knocked on the door and told the Duke's people they were there for the interview . . . and they hoped the Duke and Duchess were ready because they didn't have a lot of time. Here's the rub: No one remembered her scheduling an interview. She just showed up and said, "Let's do it." You couldn't slight her on confidence!

A TV superstar, Dorothy got bags of fan mail every day. At least one came with her photo as the address, and it still got to her! She tried to answer as many as she could, and that meant a lot of extra hours on the job. And that didn't mean she agreed with everyone. You could write her a few lines criticizing something she said on the air and you'd get back twelve pages telling you why you were wrong.

WEWS had its stars, but Dorothy Fuldheim was among its brightest. Rumors started flying in 1957 about Dorothy hosting a show for so-called "club ladies." The station figured women's clubs and church groups could be in the studio audience, have

The *One O'Clock Club* offered live entertainment and an inexpensive but elegant lunch to groups who visited the WEWS studios. Here, pianist Van Cliburn is interviewed by the show's co-host, Dorothy Fuldheim. *Cleveland Press, author's collection*

some lunch, and be entertained by Dorothy. Those rumors became reality in August with the premiere of *The One O'Clock Club*.

It was based on a show out of Cincinnati hosted by Ruth Lyons, that city's version of Dorothy. It was also syndicated to other cities and nearby states, and even a young David Letterman was a fan in Indiana.

It wasn't just Dorothy droning on about any number of topics. They had local and national acts, and at the very least the folks that showed up got a nice lunch. Ronnie Barrett led the band, and Alan Douglas was the booth announcer, though he would be replaced by Ron Penfound, who seemed to work an endless day. Co-host Bill Gordon seemed to click pretty well with Dorothy, although with both of them being so headstrong, there was initially a clash of egos about who would take what role. Sometimes the arguments went right up to air time. The formula worked. Channel 5 promoted the

No one turned down an interview with Dorothy Fuldheim! "Big Red" is seen here (with WEWS employee John Richards) reviewing footage of her interview with Pope John XXIII. *Cleveland Press, author's collection*

show as "Bill and Dorothy—terrific together!" Just a year later the show had hosted five hundred women's groups and twenty-five thousand people. It was able to draw some big name guests, too: Victor Borge, Danny Thomas, Henny Youngman, and Joe Louis, among many others. Even so, it was a lot of work for Dorothy, who eventually gave Bill Gordon more of a role so she could concentrate on news. Ticket requests never let up, and a lot of men started showing up to see what their wives were talking about. Plus, you got lunch for a dollar and a half. It was a cash cow for Channel 5 until *The Mike Douglas Show* brought it all crashing down.

Dorothy didn't show a hard edge on the show, but she could bring it out at the snap of a finger. Lawrence Spivak found out the hard way. Spivak was best known for his time on *Meet the Press*, and he came through town for a panel discussion at the Temple on

Face-off with Fuldheim. No stranger to controversy, Dorothy Fuldheim wasn't afraid to ask tough questions on live TV. Here she grills Ariane Sheppard about her husband, Dr. Sam, and the murder that put him behind bars. *Cleveland Press Collection, Cleveland State University Archives*

the Heights in Cleveland Heights. He appeared on WEWS to plug the appearance and found out that he and Dorothy didn't share the same news philosophy. Dorothy asked him straight out, "Are you a conservative or a radical?" Needless to say, Spivak protested the line of questioning but eventually declared himself an "old-fashioned liberal" who was disappointed in the controversial Secretary of State, John Foster Dulles. The conversation went on about Spivak's thoughts about Russia, Israel, and U.S. Senator Joseph McCarthy, and eventually touched on their individual styles of reporting. Dorothy asked whether Spivak did much preparation before an interview. "You can't have a first-rate interview unless you know all about the man," he said. "I'll bet I can learn a lot from your techniques, though." Dorothy looked him straight in the eye and said, "Mr. Spivak, you're soft-soaping me!"

When WEWS decided to reboot the news division in 1958, Dorothy made it clear that she reported to no one and she was her own boss. That seemed to suit the management. They also treated her differently in public than behind the scenes. In public they always referred to her as Miss Fuldheim, though in private the staff called her Dorothy. She also had another nickname that was never repeated in front of her: Mother Superior.

Dorothy also knew how to pull rank, and some people didn't like it. Nobody traveled by jet in 1958. It was too expensive, and airline travel was nowhere near as popular as it is today. Some industry bigwigs wanted Dorothy to show how fast and convenient jet travel could be, so they put her on a plane on a Sunday morning in November and flew her and a cameraman to New York. From there the two switched over to a Pan Am flight to London, where they had tea with Beatrice Lillie and did interviews with Julie Andrews and Rex Harrison. On Tuesday morning they were on the plane heading to Idewild Airport in New York, and then to Burke Lakefront, as Dorothy was expected to do her commentary that night on WEWS. That looked pretty good on paper, but there were a few snags. There was no problem with the flight. It only took six hours between New York and United Kingdom, but there was heavy fog. The plane got diverted to Shannon Airport in Ireland until receiving the all-clear to head to England. They got the interviews, jumped on the plane, and arrived in New York. Since Pan Am was footing the bill and wanted to get Dorothy home in time to edit the story, they made sure she got off the plane first. That didn't sit well with one of the passengers, who threw a fit! Zsa Zsa Gabor started screaming that she was the biggest star on board and should have been able to get off the plane before anyone else. Most of the passengers agreed she was the biggest something on board.

Even her closest friends would say you didn't mess with Dorothy. People loved her, in part, because she demanded respect. She once stopped a taping of *Polka Varieties* to chew out a saxophone player who was wearing jeans. And let's not forget her face-off with Jerry Rubin. He'd been in the news a lot since calling for anarchy during the 1968 Democratic Convention, but by 1970 Rubin discovered that you still had to play the game to sell books, and that's how he

Politicians recognized the power of Cleveland's grande dame. Here Mayor Ralph Perk salutes La Fuldheim. By the way, that's his suit, not a test pattern. *Cleveland Press, author's collection*

found himself sitting with Dorothy Fuldheim. He was pushing a book titled *Do It!* and before the show Dorothy tried to do a pre-interview. But Rubin wasn't cooperating. Dorothy wasn't about to put up with any nonsense from a Yippie or whatever he called himself and stuck a finger in his face. "If you're expecting to create a scene, I won't permit it." Rubin just smiled ear to ear and waited for the red light to go on.

It was a fight from the start. Dorothy asked why Rubin called police pigs. She said a lot of her friends were police, and Rubin shot back that a lot of his friends were Black Panthers. Then he tried to show a picture of a nude woman in the book, and Dorothy stopped him, saying it was obscene. "What's obscene about that?" Dorothy came to the end of her rope. She slammed the book shut and threw him off the set. Rubin didn't know what hit him! Guards showed him to the door, and Dorothy was a hero. Some folks didn't buy it. Bill Barrett at the *Cleveland Press* thought Dorothy had planned the confrontation, but "Big Red" denied it, saying she wouldn't put up with Rubin's "intellectual excrement."

Rubin's pal Abbie Hoffman heard what had happened and did things a little differently. When he came to Cleveland to plug his book, he greased his long hair back and wore a skinny tie that was way out of style. Dorothy warned him, "You heard what happened to your friend. I'm not going to put up with any nonsense!" Hoffman just smiled and said, "Yes, sir." In fact, he kept answering Dorothy's questions with "Yes, sir" and "No, sir" and by the end of the interview even Dorothy was laughing. Jerry Rubin later toned down his image and became a millionaire businessman. He wrote another book and found himself back in Cleveland speaking with Dorothy, who warned him right off the bat, "You remember what happened the last time you were here!" It was a lot calmer this time around.

Not everything Dorothy Fuldheim said turned to gold. Just a few weeks after she first met with Rubin, the May 4th shootings at Kent State claimed four students. Dorothy did a live report at the corner of Water and Main in Kent and blasted the Ohio National Guard. The shootings really affected her, and she even wept on the air. But it didn't affect some parts of the audience the same way. Hundreds of people called WEWS to complain, and some even came down to protest in front the station. Dorothy was pretty shaken up and offered her resignation, but the management said, "No way!"

She also took some serious flak when she interviewed a former Euclid judge who was accused in the death of his wife. Robert Steele was accused of the contract killing of his wife Marlene in 1969. He denied any involvement and went on Dorothy's show to stress his innocence. When the cameras started rolling, Dorothy told Steele to relax, but he broke down in tears. She told him, "I don't blame

This envelope speaks for itself. Dorothy Fuldheim was so well known that you didn't even need an address to get your fan mail delivered to her. *Cleveland Press, author's collection*

you at all," and Steele continued sobbing, "I love you so much. This isn't just talk. You don't know how many times Barbara [his present wife] and my mom and dad and I have talked on how wonderful you were to us." Red flag! Could this be seen as bias? The interview continued with Dorothy saying, "I hope profoundly that the real murderer will be found . . . which will then completely free you." That wasn't in the cards. Steele and two brothers, Martin and Owen Kilbane, were indicted three days later. As expected, Steele pleaded not guilty and was released on bond, but all three were later found guilty in Marlene Steele's death.

Some applauded Dorothy's comments, while others said she was too sympathetic. To the critics, Dorothy shot back: "I don't know what I could have done differently." There was even talk of a change of venue because of that interview, but Dorothy brushed it off, saying it would have no influence. She said if Steele was responsible, he should be convicted like any other murderer. But she also pointed out that, "Before I'm a news person, I'm a human being. I'm not out for blood. I want to get a story from the people I interview. I want to get information. I treat them as if they were guests in my home. He had not been arrested when I talked to him. The law says a person is presumed innocent until proved guilty. I am not a judge." It still left a bad taste for a lot of people.

Dorothy didn't have time to read all the books that came her way, so she interviewed a lot of authors and personalities cold. She could make it work . . . most of the time. Joe Namath was the New York Jets' star quarterback, but he got in a snit and stormed out of the studio when Big Red asked, "Mr. Namath, what do you do?" There was another incident with Wilt Chamberlain. Dorothy asked him point-blank why dribbling a basketball would make him worth millions of dollars.

Bill Gordon recalled another awkward exchange. It happened during a talk with Cleveland Browns place kicker Lou "The Toe" Groza on *The One O'Clock Club*. Dorothy asked, "So how high do you kick it?" Gordon jumped in to say, "You don't ask how high! It's how far. You must not know much about football." Dorothy shot back, "I find football boring! I never go in the kitchen, I don't cook or clean, and I never watch football." Maybe they should have talked about flowers.

We put people like Dorothy Fuldheim on pedestals, but we often forget that they're just like us. Dorothy would have an occasional nip and liked the way Linn Sheldon mixed her rum and cokes. Plus, she did a lot of media interviews. Johnny Carson, Phil Donahue, Barbara Walters, Ted Koppel . . . the list goes on. They loved Dorothy, in part, because she had had such a long and distinguished career, but let's face it, in a lot of ways she was a novelty. Eighty years plus and still on TV. Although she had no problem with the local folks, she was always nervous about the network interviews. To help her get over the jitters, general manager Don Perris would keep a few beers on hand so she could knock one back before the interview. She didn't get smashed. It just took off the edge. When she was out of town she was on her own.

The comedian Richard Pryor was not a fan, at least at first. They were both guests on *The Tonight Show,* and it was nothing new to Dorothy. It was her fourth time, and she was pretty relaxed. Maybe too relaxed. At one point she said stories about poverty and prejudice in America were overblown, and Pryor's eyebrows shot into his scalp. He challenged her right away, but Dorothy came right back and said, "The U.S. may have its bad spots, but there

Dorothy Fuldheim could ad-lib her way through most interviews, but would occasionally find time to do some homework before air time. *Cleveland Press, author's collection*

is no one starving or sleeping in the streets like in India. No one has to starve here." At this point Pryor's jaw dropped. He let loose a tsunami of words hinting but never saying the words *prejudice* or *racial bias*. Dorothy knew what was happening, so to ease the tension she held Pryor's hand for the rest of the exchange. Everyone had a laugh and parted friends. Other prominent names saw the other side of Dorothy as well. She once did a spot on ABC's *Good Morning America*, and David Hartman loved her. He said, "Dorothy, I could talk to you for an hour. Would you come back and talk with us some more?" Dorothy shot back, "No! You kept me waiting a half an hour downstairs. If you want to talk to me, you can come to Cleveland!"

Dorothy let you know when she didn't like something. Gib Shanley recalled her coming into the Channel 5 newsroom and slamming her purse on a desk. She yelled out, "I hate banks!" Gib asked why, and she said her building was going condo, and they had offered her and the other tenants a chance to buy their apartments. Now keep in mind that Dorothy could have afforded to buy the whole building, so why she went to a bank is anyone's guess. Even though she was well into her seventies when this happened, they kept trying to get Dorothy to sign a twenty-five year mortgage!

By the way, on more than one occasion Dorothy finished her commentary and walked away from the set . . . right in front of Gib Shanley during his sports segment. After this happened a couple of times he returned the compliment by loosening his tie, lighting a cigarette, and walking in front of Dorothy during her commentary. Even though she seemed out of touch at times, Dorothy made international headlines when she signed a three-year contract at the age of ninety.

Dorothy Fuldheim wanted to work until she could work no more, and that day finally arrived in July 1984. She had spoken to popes, presidents, and just about every world leader, and her last interview was via satellite with Ronald Reagan. There were problems before the interview. Dorothy didn't look right but wanted to do it. GM Don Perris was in the control room and realized during the exchange with Reagan that something was wrong. He would later say he should never have allowed her to go ahead with the interview. It was her final assignment at WEWS. Dorothy did her commentary that night at 6 p.m. and shortly after, suffered a major stroke.

You can't say Dorothy Fuldheim didn't love what she did, though some would say she did it too long. But why did she push herself for such a long time? Maybe she didn't even know. Let's go back to that conversation with the Duke of Windsor. After their interview he asked Dorothy, "Do you do this often?" and she answered yes. When he asked why, Dorothy shrugged and said, "To pay the rent!"

From Fanny Bumps to the Director's Chair

Women in Television

IF YOU WERE LOOKING for two words to describe early television, they would be "racist" and "sexist." That's the way society was back then, and TV reflected it. We're not saying that's right. That's just the way it was, and we've come a long way since. Blacks and women were cast in stereotyped roles, and there weren't many opportunities beyond that. Dorothy Fuldheim was the exception, and she had a great reputation long before she landed at WEWS. The glass ceiling was a foot thick, and few jobs were available for women, especially on screen. Even so, some were able force their way in. Betty Cope was one of them. She was working for an ad agency when she switched over to write copy at Channel 5 for $160 a month.

TV was the ultimate boys' club, and Betty saw it first hand. If you were working your way up the ladder you had to win respect, and that wasn't easy. Tom Piskura told the story that Channel 5 was supplying a link with the Cleveland Indians for the *Ed Sullivan Show* in New York. The camera would pan from left to right, top to bottom, and the announcer would name each player. The introductions didn't match the players, and Ed hit the roof on live TV. "Get your act together, Cleveland!" Betty Cope was the contact at WEWS, and an engineer at CBS control in New York yelled into the headset, "What do you expect from a goddamn woman?"

Alice Weston came about a year later to host a show for women. It became so popular she was offered a network show but turned it down because "family came first." This was a major victory for

Cleveland was a pioneer city in welcoming women to work in TV. Here, Janet Henry checks out WEWS's Betty Cope, who would later go on to start the city's public television station. *Cleveland Press, author's collection*

Alice because when she was a kid, she had such a bad lisp that no one could understand her. She had corrective surgery, and her dad coached her in public speaking. It was a major roadblock, but Alice was able to overcome it with a lot of hard work (and a few stitches). Her name was actually Alice Showalter, but she changed her last name so it was closer to the call letters, WEWS.

We all remember Paige Palmer. She was able to get her foot in the door, but it wasn't easy. Paige was running a charm school out of an old broken down house in Akron, and she was so down and out that her friends had to chip in to get it repaired. Some time back she had won a beauty contest and posed for "naughty but nice" calendar paintings, but those didn't pay that well. Paige had a few other fashion-related jobs, and then the call came from Betty Cope, who was now in the programming department. Like

Before Rachel Ray or Giada De Laurentiis were even born, Alice Weston was breaking new ground as a TV chef. *Cleveland Press, author's collection*

Alice Weston, they offered her a ladies' show with fashion tips and exercises that were pretty much a waste of time. Most of them centered on bumping your butt up and down on an exercise mat. Or you could pull huge rubber bands to tone up flabby arms . . . all available by mail order through "Paige Palmer's Exercise Equipment." For many years Paige also smoked four packs of cigarettes a day.

Betty Cope would become one of the most respected women in broadcasting, but that respect came with a lot of bumps and bruises. Paige Palmer was too sick to work one week, and Betty filled in, doing the whole show, including the fanny bumps. At the end of the week she was walking on Euclid Avenue and a couple of full-figured women stopped to say hello. Betty thought they wanted an autograph. Instead they told her, "We love it when you do the exercises because you can't do them either!" Paige, Betty, Alice, and Dorothy Fuldheim were among the few women that had jobs of any substance on screen.

Most of the technical jobs were taken by men. Women had a chance in clerical jobs or even cooking segments, but after that it was slim pickings. It was such a novelty that Betty Cope stumped the panel on CBS's *What's My Line?* when they failed to guess her job as a TV director. The comedian Steve Allen was on that panel, and he couldn't guess Cope's occupation even though he worked with her when he did a promotional appearance at WEWS!

Cleveland Press writer Nancy Gallagher decided to explore TV from the other side of the lens when she approached WEWS director Betty Cope about trying camera work for a show. Cope agreed to let Gallagher handle one of two cameras for the *Paige Palmer Show*. Gallagher wrote that camera man Bill Wiedenman had warned her that one of the hardest things for a beginner to master is control of the situation. "If the mike boom creeps onto the screen, just don't stand there and laugh," Wiedenman said. "Move the camera so the picture is centered and everything is where it should be." With that, Gallagher began her "baptism by fire." She put on a headset to receive instructions from Cope, who told Palmer not to stand up too quickly in front of the fledgling videographer because her head might be cut off in the picture. Gallagher also executed some extreme zooms on Palmer that might have confused the home audience, not to mention the writer herself. At one point she even caught Palmer's leotard creeping up, and the director switched to a more modest angle. At the end of the program, Palmer and Wiedenman thanked Gallagher for her interest but advised her to stick to newspaper work.

Channel 5 did air a show in the late '50s called *Courage*. It had an interesting hook. The show was hosted by Kathleen King, who was blind. She just described how people with handicaps could lead normal lives. King showed how to do household chores, such as ironing clothes and cooking, and wanted to do commercials that tied into her blindness. The local ad agencies thought that

Paige Palmer had a long-time daily show on WEWS that emphasized fashion and fitness. This photo shows Palmer with Canadian TV fitness expert Ed Allen. *Cleveland Press Collection, Cleveland State University Archives*

was taking it a bit too far. They didn't want the station to be seen as capitalizing on her handicap.

Then there was Laura Lane. Laura came to Channel 5 saying she wanted to be the station's fashion editor. She had been a model and had written for magazines, so she seemed qualified. The station hired Laura, but not for the job she wanted. One night in the fall of 1958 they put her on after the station's late-night movie. They had her curled up on a couch in a flimsy outfit describing how to go to sleep. The director said he wanted "demure and alluring" and played cocktail music in the background. It lasted one night. Years later Laura said, "No rehearsals! I didn't even know what camera to look at!" Plus, there were so many complaints even for that hour that it got yanked from the schedule. The next night they ran the test pattern. No complaints!

There was a rising star out of Columbus who wouldn't get famous until she left Channel 5. Everyone knew Dody Goodman had talent. She was even a regular on Jack Paar's *Tonight Show*. They just couldn't find a place for her when she moved back to Ohio. She had a great sense of comedy, and in the early '60s WEWS gave Goodman a one-week try-out on the *One O'Clock Club*. It was weird. She went from table to table, getting impromptu comments about Dorothy Fuldheim's news commentary. She was no Bill Gordon. She couldn't ad lib, and some of Goodman's comments made you shake your head. Here's an example: Dorothy did a report about illegitimate children, and Goodman came back with, "I don't believe in illegitimate children, but somebody should look after them just like legitimate ones!" Huh?! Goodman bounced around the station for a few weeks and eventually made it out to Hollywood, where she struck gold. She won roles on dozens of shows, including *Diff'rent Strokes* and *Search for Tomorrow*, but most people remember her as Mary's ditzy mom Martha Shumway on *Mary Hartman, Mary Hartman*. She pretty much played that role in real life in Cleveland.

Norma Quarles deserves a mention here, too. In July 1967 she signed on as a general assignment reporter with the NBC News Bureau at WKYC-TV. Quarles, who began her career in Chicago, traveled to New York in 1966 to train in the NBC news department. It was a baptism by fire. One reporter told the news director he couldn't send her to cover a hippie disturbance in Harlem: "You cannot send her into that! She's a woman!" The news director shot back, "She is not! She is a reporter." She did fine, nabbing a five-minute newscast at WKYC at 1:25 each afternoon. Norma's star would continue to rise all the way to the NBC network.

The Ultimate Amateur Hour

Gene Carroll

YOU NEVER GOT THE impression that Gene Carroll had ever been a young man. Gene always looked like an old codger, even in his publicity photos from the 1930s when he was part of the "Gene and Glenn" radio show with Glenn Rowell. By the time TV came around and he started at WEWS you thought, "This guy isn't buying any green bananas." But he had lots of young fans who called him "Uncle Jake." Then again, his co-host was only five years old.

Gene's *Uncle Jake's House*, Cleveland TV's first kids' program, went on the air in April 1948, and there were plenty of imitators that followed, including King Jupiter, Pat Dopp the Play Lady, Mr. Banjo, *Charming Children*, and Tom Haley's robot sidekick, Mr. Rivitz. They all wanted a piece of the kids' show pie (and the advertising that came with it) but Uncle Jake was the first out of the box, and he ran with it. Advertisers found out that TV put products right in front of the audience, and kids were an easy target. His biggest sponsor was Bosco Chocolate Syrup . . . and Uncle Jake sold a lot of Bosco!

Gene had an interesting background. He was born in Chicago in 1897 and got the acting bug early on. His dad wanted him to sell insurance, but Gene wouldn't have it. He dropped out of school to do vaudeville, and that's how he met his first love. Virginia McMath was part of an all-girl troupe called the "Texas Redheads," and Gene was with her every minute they weren't on stage. But her mom was no fan of Gene Carroll and brought any possible romance to a screeching halt. Virginia McMath would later change her name and hit the big time as Ginger Rogers. He eventually made his way to Cleveland.

You're not seeing double. Gene Carroll (on harmonica) promotes his *Giant Tiger Amateur Hour* along with Blanche Allritton and Vince Haydock on ukulele. That's Gene again on the end, as Uncle Jake, the kids' show host. *Author's Collection, Cleveland Press*

It wasn't long before radio was in every home, and by 1930 Gene had a hit show with his partner Glenn Rowell as "Gene and Glenn" on WTAM. It had stock characters like Jake and Lena (who were both played by Gene), and the show was so popular that by 1934 it was picked up by NBC. He had a big influence during his days in radio. The great Jack Benny told a New York newspaper that he was he was doing well on the vaudeville stage, but "Gene and Glenn" inspired him to get into radio, and he never looked back. The act stayed together until 1943, when Rowell went into war work and Gene took a role on NBC radio's *Fibber McGee and Molly*. Gene also had no problem meeting the ladies. In fact, he was married three times by 1940, but the last marriage, to Helen Olsen, was a keeper. She was with him until he died.

One of the first TV kids show hosts in the country, Gene Carroll's "Uncle Jake" was also one of the first to market specialty items, such as his signature hat. *Cleveland Public Library*

By 1948 the Carrolls were back in Cleveland to stay. They started a talent school, and Gene got his foot in the door early at WEWS. Even though a lot of people didn't have TVs, it was still a selling point to get people signed up for the school. Gene started a program in April 1948 showcasing amateur talent. It was named after the sponsor, the *Giant Tiger Amateur Hour*, after the discount stores with the logo that looked suspiciously like Tony the Tiger. The problem was, most of the alleged talent was pretty much the same. Off-key singers, tap dancers, and an endless parade of accordion players, though it did show a little more variety as the series went on. It aired Sunday mornings when most people went to church or were nursing hangovers from the night before. Needless to say, the accordion players didn't win a lot of fans for the folks looking for "the hair of the dog." But Gene also had Uncle Jake to fall back on . . . and a secret weapon.

Uncle Jake's House was one of the first kids' programs to air live anywhere in the country. Gene also had a co-host named Candy Lee, who was five years old when the show first went on the air.

Candy remembers, "My career began in 1945 when I won first prize in a local beauty contest. I'd been singing around the house and memorizing poems, so my mom worked at getting me out on the stage and getting publicity. She took me to a voice coach, Gayle Gaylord, who had a studio in the Arcade and taught voice, drama radio announcing, theatrical makeup, and more. I was there from April to July 1946. The problem was, she was totally oriented toward adults. I believe she recommended me to Gene because he had a studio in the Citizens Building and offered more for children."

Candy says Gene knew about her when she walked in the door. "My press clippings were not lost on Gene, and in 1947 he got me a Screen Children's Guild Card and entered me in their Little Miss America Contest in California. I came in second! While I was there for the contest Gene called his old pal Bob Hope, and he invited my mom and I [*sic*] to his home. I played with his kids, and he gave my mom a script for me to learn for a part in *Sorrowful Jones*."

But that first step to the movies hit a snag. Candy recalls, "We stayed at the Drake Hotel. There was a switchboard, of course, and we would get hand-written messages showing who called. In June 1948, Jay Kanter called. He was a very ambitious agent at MCA who went on to be the agent for Marilyn Monroe, Grace Kelly, and Marlon Brando. He had a perfect role for me in a movie, and I had to be at the studio the next day. The only problem was, I had just been diagnosed with chicken pox and was confined to the hotel room for a week!"

Candy and her mom spent six months in California waiting for the next big break before heading back to Cleveland.

Candy says, "The first months of *Uncle Jake's House* were all about establishing Gene Carroll to a new and younger audience.

Always a showman . . . and a promoter! Gene Carroll became so popular with the *Giant Tiger Amateur Hour* that the show eventually just assumed his name and became *The Gene Carroll Show. Cleveland Public Library*

I was only five, but I had the press clippings and some talent, so Gene chose me to be on *Uncle Jake's House* with him. I doubt he really had any plan for the show except to continue his show-biz career and add his character derived from Jake and Lena." Candy also admits his fascination with little kids might seem a little weird in today's world, but it was a far more innocent time. Just a few years later a New York psychologist named Dr. Frederic Wertham would raise red flags with parents across the country with questions raised in his book *Seduction of the Innocent.* The book claimed comic books and even some early TV caused juvenile delinquency, and it questioned Batman's living arrangements with his teenage assistant, Robin.

So what about the other kids who would occasionally appear with Uncle Jake and her? Candy says, "I honestly don't remember how the kids got on the show. They were just there when I arrived at the studio. I would guess they phoned in. Gene's wife, Helen, was the brains behind the studio and parts of the show. I would guess that was her department."

The show was an instant hit due, in part, to being the first of its kind. It also drew a lot of interest off the screen.

Candy recalls, "We did a lot of personal appearances, both together and separately, but one of the biggest was at the Palace Theatre, thanks to another of Gene's old pals, Max Mink, who owned the Palace. Max and Gene signed the contract on the golf course. We were on stage in person with 'Uncle Jake's Party' along with Disney cartoons. We also did shows at the Keith's 105th Street Theater." Then there was an appearance at Kelley's Island in 1949. Nature was apparently not a fan of Uncle Jake. "I just remember trying to get the Canadian soldiers [the bugs] out of my mouth as I was singing!" Candy believes she did as many as 250 consecutive appearances on *Uncle Jake's House* in a little over a year.

It was a different time for kids back then. By 1952 there were a lot of programs on the air, and children were an important audience. But the kids' shows didn't have the special effects and big budgets that would come later on. Some of them, such as *Breakfast Party* and *Charming Tots* on WNBK, were instructional. The audience played games and saw puppet shows. Cowboys and the Old West were familiar themes, so you had *Gabby Hayes, Buckskin Billy*, and the ratings magnet, *Howdy Doody*, after school. It was pretty much the same thing over at WEWS, with Bob Dale playing a Civil War vet named Tim Twitter and Jim Breslin as Texas Jim. Gene Carroll's Uncle Jake was like a member of the family. An early fan was Don Novello, who remembered a photo of Gene and Glenn that his grandparents kept in the family album. He fondly recalls Uncle Jake going down his imaginary elevator to feed his dogs in the basement.

Candy spent some quality time with Uncle Jake's show, but she and her parents thought it was time for a change. She left the show in 1950 but was still in demand on the kids' circuit. She recalls, "Walt 'Kousin' Kay was working at WXEL, and when I was

"Don't work with kids or animals!" Gene Carroll never took that advice, and it didn't hurt his career one bit. The young lady in the beret is Andrea DeCapite, one of Carroll's students, who would later have a hit with the song "Please Don't Talk to the Lifeguard." She took the stage name Andrea Carroll in tribute to Gene.
Cleveland Public Library

leaving *Uncle Jake's House* Walt kind of pounced. He proposed that I appear with him on his TV show. I had name recognition, and he knew it could help build his audience. Walt and I did a ton of appearances together and even recorded a record, 'Kousin Kay Polka' and 'Buy Me One More Ice Cream Cone.' We did appearances, too, at the Park and Granada theaters for one-hour shows."

Rivalries aside, the Carrolls and Candy's family remained close. "Gene and Helen and my parents and I were friends and would often get together. When invited to my parents' house for dinner, Gene would always ask my mom to make her double-breaded pork chops. That was kind of an interesting request from a Jewish boy from Chicago! I felt badly [*sic*] when Gene passed away two days after my daughter was born, that he never got to see her. However, I did make an appearance at the 1973 anniversary show and sang while holding my daughter."

Gene and Linn Sheldon were long-time friends since the early days at WEWS. They had a similar sense of humor and were quick to show it. Linn remembered a formal event at Public Hall back in the early 1950s. The date and even the reason for the event escaped him, but he remembered sitting at a table on the main floor with Gene and his wife. Gene left for a few minutes, and when he got back, there was an announcement from the stage that Rocky Marciano, heavyweight champion of the world, was in attendance. The spotlights swung around and focused on Linn, who stood up waving with his hand in front of his face. The jokes kept going back and forth, and after dinner the dessert trays came by. There was only one piece of Boston cream pie, and Gene and Linn both had their eye on it. Linn excused himself to use the restroom, and when he came back, there was a note from Gene on the pie that said, "I spit on this." When Gene left for a pit stop he came back to find another note that said, "Me, too!"

Trends change, kids grow up, and by the mid-1950s Uncle Jake was replaced by younger guys such as Linn Sheldon's Uncle Leslie and Ron Penfound's Captain Penny. Gene's amateur show was still going strong, but one show a week wasn't paying all the bills. Plus, other talent schools were bringing in students for the amateur hour, so the variety show didn't depend exclusively on Gene's talent pool. But he had an idea to generate some extra cash. In July 1956 he started a production company to produce special effects for TV. Gene first met Del Thomas when he built a seven-foot wooden lamp post and carted it across town by bus so Gene could check it out. They got to work building custom scenery for all the WEWS shows and decided they would go into special effects. They were state-of-the-art for that time. For the weather forecasts they would drop soap chips or corn flakes or, if they really wanted to wow the sponsors, superimpose dots on a second camera. Fog was dry ice and hot water, and rain came from a sprinkling can.

Gene did some specials for the Landmark Company and was able to attract some big-name entertainers like Bob Hope. Even so, he was best known for the *Giant Tiger Amateur Hour*. By his tenth year on the air, in April 1958, he'd done 520 shows. With eight acts per show, he enabled more than 4,000 to get time on the screen. Plus, he was still in his original time slot of noon to 1 p.m. on Sundays. He even had some break-out acts. Andrea DeCapite was two-and-a-half when she started with the show in 1949 and was still on the air in 1972. Andrea would have hits with "I've Got a Date with Elvis" and, later, "Please Don't Talk to the Lifeguard." She was no relation to Gene but changed her stage name to Andrea Carroll as a tribute to him.

Since everything was a first in those early days of TV, occasionally there would be a glitch. Gene had the public write in to judge the acts and would give a prize to the winning performer every thirteen weeks. The flaws in that plan are obvious. If you had a lot of friends and family you got a lot of votes. The straw that broke the camel's back was when the kid who played harmonica beat out a dancer who went on to a big career as a Radio City Music Hall Rockette.

The *Giant Tiger Amateur Hour* became the *Gene Carroll Show* in the mid-'60s, and he stayed on as host until his death in 1972. Gene never really recovered from a heart attack he suffered at his vacation home in Florida that March. As he was lying in the hospital bed, his wife said, "It was lucky this didn't happen on the golf course." Gene snapped back with, "If I'd been playing golf it wouldn't have happened!" He taped enough shows to run through May, and his final one ran the day he died. WEWS tried to keep the franchise going with radio host Jim Runyon, who died a short time later, and then Don Webster. It wasn't the same without Gene Carroll, and the show was cancelled. Gene couldn't be replaced. The other guys just seemed too young.

When You Didn't Have Another Program . . .

Movie Hosts

MOVIES AND EARLY TV were a match made in heaven. They took up a lot of air time, there was little editing, and you could put them on any time of the day—and stations did just that. You could see a movie at one in the morning, the *Milkman's Matinee* (as if milkmen would get up extra early to see a film). They would also air in early afternoon, late morning, or any time of day when you didn't have another program. It was like a theater in your home, and you didn't have to pay admission. The station just had to fit the movie around commercials. That was Lawson Deming's job.

Lawson was hired by WNBK right out of Cleveland College in 1949. He was a voice actor, but he also did a lot of technical work. One of his jobs was to edit films for time. He would take 16 mm movies home to his editing suite, and his family got to watch movies right in their own living room. But as host of the afternoon *One O'Clock Playhouse*, he got some very strange fan letters. An old lady wrote to say she got dressed up for the show every day because, knowing Lawson could see her through the tube, she wanted to look her best. He contacted her family and found out what she was going to wear on her birthday. When the show aired Lawson made it a point to compliment her on the beautiful pink frock. Her response? The woman turned around and yelled, "There! I told you he could see me!"

Then there was Jim Breslin at WEWS. He played this grizzled old prospector named Texas Jim and would host the cowboy movies and tell "tales from the Old West" during the breaks. In

KYW's "Big" Wilson had no idea just how difficult a real wallaby could be when he took one on as a mascot for *The Early Show* in 1958. *Cleveland Press, author's collection*

the mid-1950s, KYW hired John "Big" Wilson for his own radio show and to host the *Six O'Clock Adventures* with Roy Rogers and Jungle Jim movies on KYW-TV. "Biggie" was six feet tall and more than three hundred pounds, and his personal story was better than the movies. For most of the year he lived on a yacht with a fireplace and crates of liquor stacked to the ceiling. Linn Sheldon came out to the marina to visit one day and brought a bag of potato chips. "Biggie" looked at him and asked, "What am I supposed to do with all this food?" He was a really personable guy who even got the attention of major show business names like Jackie Cooper. He flew him out to Hollywood to try out for the lead in a TV series called *Fat Man*, but Screen Gems passed. He still had plenty of work in Cleveland.

"Big" was a born promoter, but some of his ideas went off the rails pretty quickly. KYW had this idea to promote togetherness. Listen to Biggie on the radio and then watch him with the family on the new *Early Show* movie at 4:30, just after Barnaby. Here's where it gets a little weird. Bob Nashick was the publicist at Channel 3, and to push the togetherness angle he came up with mascots, a kangaroo and her joey in the pouch . . . and he insisted it had to be a live kangaroo! When the station saw how big a kangaroo was, Nashick thought a wallaby might be a little more manageable. In fact, they could call it the "K-Y-Wallaby"! "Biggie" didn't want the animal to be nervous when they introduced it on TV, so he said it could live with him for a couple of weeks. Nashick flew to New York to talk to the Australian consulate, and after a couple of weeks (and $200 under the table) the wallaby arrived at Big's doorstep. He wasn't about to change his lifestyle, and neither was the wallaby. It wasn't house-trained, so Big slipped and slid his way across the room to the liquor. He brought the wallaby to the station, but it had no intention of appearing on TV. It wouldn't go near the cameras. The management threw up its hands and called the Cleveland Zoo for a pickup.

That didn't hurt Big Wilson. He was as popular as ever, and KYW would even let him dump movies for a live show every now and then. It was the first time Tom Conway (later Tim) appeared on screen, and if there were stars in town they'd come in and do skits, too. The real story was Tim Conway.

Tim left Channel 3 for a job at WJW. At the same time, Ernie Anderson had switched over from WHK radio to Channel 8, and in 1961 the station debuted *Ernie's Place*. It went on early, about 9:30 in the morning, but those were also the days of stay-at-home moms, so the target audience was pretty obvious. Tim and Ernie had been friends and started doing comedy skits between the movie segments. That's where they got into trouble.

In 1980 Tim told WERE's Ken Prewitt, "We went to Channel 8 and sold Ernie as talent and myself as a director. He had never been talent, and I had never been directing! I never learned to back-time the pictures, so when the program was over, the movie ended at the same time. We just kind of faded out a lot of times before the movies ended. We would show the ends of the movies on Friday! That lasted about two weeks before people found out we weren't doing all that well. Ernie also wanted to have guests, but I couldn't get anyone to come on, so I would be the guest. He would say, 'Here's a bullfighter. Here's a trumpet player. Here's whatever.' I would come out and be the guest. It was out of necessity that I became a performer!" It wasn't long before he was performing on a much larger stage.

The actress Rose Marie came to Cleveland that August to promote *The Dick Van Dyke Show*, and she liked the stuff Tim and Ernie were doing. She took a film of them to Ed Sullivan to see if he would put them on his Sunday night show, but he turned them down. Steve Allen was a different story. He loved them, but he could only use Tim Conway since he, too, played the straight man. Although Tim had a hard choice to make, Ernie made it easy on him. He told Tim he would be crazy to pass up that chance, and to call if there was an opportunity for him later on. By November Tim was a regular on *The Steve Allen Show* and Rose Marie was his personal manager. He was also doing material that Ernie Anderson helped to write.

Tim was hoping for a series so he could persuade Ernie to leave Cleveland for the West Coast. Meanwhile, Channel 8 kept Ernie Anderson on his toes. Along with booth announcing and *Ernie's Place*, they put him to work hosting different shows and documentaries. When after a few months Steve Allen suspended production of his show, Tim Conway returned to *Ernie's Place* . . . at least for a while. He got a call about a new show called *McHale's Navy*, starring Ernest Borgnine, and the rest is TV history.

Something else happened in 1963 that would change Cleveland TV forever.

Universal Studios was making its monster movies available to TV packaged under the name *Shock Theater*. These were the classics! Frankenstein, the Wolfman, the Mummy—all the characters that gave kids nightmares twenty years before were now coming

"Mad Daddy" Pete Myers was Cleveland's original horror movie host back in 1958. This promotional photo (with Madeline Swim) would draw plenty of unwanted attention today. *Cleveland Press, author's collection*

right into their living rooms. The syndicator suggested local stations get a host to introduce the films. WJW offered Ernie an extra $75 a week, and the legend was born. This was not a new concept. Pete "Mad Daddy" Myers had had a huge audience on WJW back in 1958 when the TV side offered him a chance to try the character on late-night TV. He could make rhymes a mile a minute and called his radio show "a bubbling pot of wavy gravy!" Mad

Daddy was supposed to be a vampire with a hood and cape, and the imagery came off a lot better listening to radio. But he also helped lay the groundwork for things to come. When Pete was on WHK he would do a two-hour show every night as "lovable, laughable Pete Myers." Then he would leave for an hour dinner break that he would drink from a martini glass and . . . BANG! He was the Mad Daddy! The guy who filled in during his break every day was Ernie Anderson.

Ernie had a pretty good voice-over career, but you made money where you could. He accepted the late-night Friday gig thinking no one would see him. Just to be sure his clients wouldn't recognize him, he pasted on a phony beard and a fright wig. Ghoulardi was born! No one tells that story better than Tom Feran and R. D. Heldenfels in their book, *Ghoulardi—Inside Cleveland TV's Wildest Ride* (Gray & Co., 1998).

Ghoulardi was the biggest star ever to come out of Cleveland TV. The show debuted in 1963, and by 1964 even the Beatles had heard about him. A reporter asked them at their September 1964 Cleveland press conference what they thought of Ghoulardi who, he mistakenly said, was the first to play their records. John Lennon asked, "Was he? A lot of people say they did." Paul McCartney simply added, "If he did, he has good taste." Ghoulardi was never accused of good taste! Plus, Ernie couldn't care less about the Beatles. He was a jazz fan and hated rock and roll. *Author's Note*: In what would be the last interview he ever did, I mentioned to Ernie that he had given one of the interns an opportunity to meet the Beatles. He gave me a sick look and said, "You call that an opportunity?"

Oddly enough, Jimmy Zero of the Dead Boys would later tell me that Cleveland was one of the few places in America that had embraced punk rock because Ghoulardi showed how much fun anarchy could be. It wasn't long before a Saturday afternoon show was added to the lineup.

Ghoulardi was 100 percent Ernie Anderson, though he did have some influences. Mad Daddy was one of them. A lot of the vocal patter and even words like "Amrap" (Parma spelled backwards) had been used by Pete Myers. There were major differences, too. Mad Daddy had some weird production demands. He wanted an eight-hundred-pound studio camera suspended from the ceiling so it looked like he was upside down. When they explained it would collapse the roof, it was Daddy upside down—though not for long. The blood would rush to his head and he would get dizzy, partly because of his three-martini dinners. Ernie was content to stay seated most of the time and occasionally move around the set or walk into the movie. But his favorite seat was at Seagram's Bar next door to Channel 8.

Seagram's was nicknamed "The Swamp." *Shock Theater* producer Chuck Schodowski recalls how Ernie used to go there quite a bit. He liked Pierre's down the street, too, and would stop in now and then for a martini and a game of dominoes with the bartender. But Seagram's was a different atmosphere. More convenient, too. Sometimes Ernie would dash over between breaks when he was doing Ghoulardi. He'd have his usual martini and keep an eye on the TV. When it was time to go to a break he'd rush down Euclid Avenue and often make it just in time to improvise a few lines before getting back into the movie. You'd see him a few minutes later stepping through the front door of Seagram's, beard and all, asking for a fresh drink and watching the screen out of the corner of his eye so he could do it all over again.

Meanwhile, Ernie Anderson's bearded juggernaut continued to roll, and WJW added a 5:00 to 5:30 p.m. *Laurel, Ghoulardi and Hardy* film segment to its daily afternoon lineup. Like the Friday show, it aimed to satisfy its audience with slapstick and commentary. Some thought that too much of a good thing might eventually wear thin, but Anderson continued to rake in big ratings and plenty of talent fees from appearances. He also had his late-night gig. Ghoulardi remained the king of horror films at Channel 8, though it wasn't the monsters that drew in viewers. It was Anderson's biting satire and wit. Ghoulardi broke rules almost daily, skewering local icons such as Linn Sheldon's Barnaby, Ron

One of the all-time superstars of Cleveland TV was Ernie Anderson as Ghoulardi. He took swipes at his many friends on other channels, and they loved him for it. Years after he left, Anderson couldn't understand the continuing appeal, even claiming it just wasn't all that funny. *Cleveland Press Collection, Cleveland State University Archives*

Penfound as Captain Penny, and the grande dame of Cleveland news, Dorothy Fuldheim. "I've never even heard of him," Fuldheim parried. "Is he the gentleman who does my beer commercials, by any chance?" Actually, all three were friends of Ernie Anderson, who would never have said anything truly hurtful about them. Anderson was so popular by then that Channel 8 forfeited a news conference by JFK for a 5 p.m. Ghoulardi show.

Ghoulardi continued to draw big numbers on TV and huge crowds for personal appearances. Another Ernest Anderson, however, was not so happy. The Shaker Heights resident had to fend off endless phone calls from fans looking for the Anderson who played their "king and leader." Of course, Channel 8's Anderson had an unlisted phone number at his Willoughby home.

Anderson saw the profit potential and soon announced plans for Ghoulardi, Inc. T-shirts and other merchandise, prompting Storer Broadcasting to petition a court to shut down that operation—especially now that Ghoulardi, a phenomenon after only seven months, was being shopped around for national syndication. He sure had the local following to back up a syndication move. The TV trade paper, *Sponsor*, noted that every week, Ghoulardi drew an audience averaging 130,000 men, 155,000 women, 104,000 teens, and even 61,200 children. The numbers were equally impressive for the Saturday afternoon show. Anderson confided that he targeted the teenage audience, saying they were always a lot hipper than adults. That fall the show was farmed out to WSPD/Toledo, where for a few weeks Anderson filmed inserts for afternoon *Maverick* reruns, but Ernie didn't think it would last and, frankly, didn't care. Word was he was having an affair with a woman there and just used the tapings as an excuse to travel to Toledo once a week.

Capitalizing on a hit, WJW expanded Ernie Anderson's Ghoulardi role to an afternoon movie. He toned down the material for the younger crowd, and the legend continued to grow at a breakneck pace. Anderson shared credit for the success of Ghoulardi with cameraman Chuck Schodowski and projectionist Bob

Soinski, who collected many of the bizarre film clips seen during the movies and breaks. The marketing potential of the character was escalating quickly, with talk of a soft drink, novelty records, and other tie-ins coming in daily.

The AFTRA walkout that hit WJW radio and TV in November 1963 caused confusion for Ghoulardi fans when Ernie Anderson joined coworkers on the picket line, but the station wasn't about to lose the audience. Management personnel filled in for striking workers on that and other live studio segments. Artist Van Timmons and development manager Bob Guy put on Ghoulardi's lab coat and beard to host the shows and fooled no one in the process.

Ernie Anderson was good at headlines, and he did it again when Parma mayor James Day took him to task over the way his "Parma Place" soap opera spoofed his community (Polish jokes were prevalent at the time). Day said the *Peyton Place* parody insulted the city by suggesting all its citizens wore white socks, had plastic pink flamingoes in their front yards, and maintained a diet of kielbasi sandwiches. Day told the *Press*, "Parma was being made to sound like a foot disease!"

Anderson said he had nothing against Parma, having lived there for a time, but he cut references to the city from episodes still in the can before retiring "Parma Place" permanently. WKYC radio's morning team of Harry Martin and "Specs" Howard took the opportunity to boost Parma's image by inviting city leaders to talk up their town, joking Parma should have its own flag and engage in a "cultural exchange" with other Northeast Ohio communities. A fraternity at Cuyahoga Community College sponsored "Parma Place a Go Go," offering free admission to the event to those wearing white socks. Some Parma residents wrote the *Press* stating they enjoyed the satirical look at their town.

Anderson didn't just sit back while the controversy raged. He tweaked his show a bit, taking advantage of the high camp and nostalgia craze ABC's *Batman* had triggered by including old Buster Crabbe *Flash Gordon* serials on his Friday and Saturday shows.

The Ghoulardi character was also heard on voice-overs for a public service campaign asking people not to jaywalk, which Anderson later said was ridiculous: "It was like telling people, 'Don't fart!'"

Ernie was an actor at heart, and in 1965 he got a chance to show his stuff, even if only for a few seconds, when the call came from CBS. *Gunsmoke* had lost a popular player that year with the departure of Dennis Weaver, aka "Chester." To fill the vacuum and ward off a ratings drop, producers asked affiliates to submit photos and bios of staff they wanted to promote as entertainers. Ernie got the nod for a show the following season. He headed out in early August after filming *Ghoulardi* segments for the Friday night shows in Cleveland.

When Ernie showed up on the *Gunsmoke* set, the makeup man told him he looked too aristocratic and began making him more grizzled. Only on set for two days—to deliver three lines—Anderson suffered through temperatures of 100-plus degrees and endured many retakes caused by loud airplanes overhead. He earned the Screen Actors Guild $299 minimum for his performance, set for the September 28 season premiere.

It was also one of the rare times Anderson would not be at the Channel 8 studios for a live Ghoulardi appearance. He had filmed segments to run between the film clips so the show could air during his time in California. The surviving film remains one of the few recordings of a Ghoulardi TV performance.

Charities often asked TV performers to help raise money, and one of the most popular—and profitable—attractions was WJW's Ghoulardi All-Stars. The team took on all comers in basketball, football, and softball, playing school faculties and professional sports teams to make thousands of dollars for the sponsoring charity. The All-Stars included staffers Jim Reynolds, Chuck Schodowski, Dom Lolli, Bob (Hoolihan) Wells, Ralph Tarsitano, Mike Wagner, Jim Doney, Chuck Lorius, Dick Lorius, Ray (Franz the Toymaker) Stawiarski, and, of course, Ernie Anderson himself. Dick Goddard joined later. Sponsors financed the All-Stars bus, and the group played up to one hundred games a year. These events often ended in parties at a bar or a home. There were parties on the bus, too, usually with a jug of homemade wine from Ralph "Papa Tarts" Tarsitano.

Here's a bit of Ghoulardi trivia: The Big Summer TV Party with Chuck McCann in the summer of 1967 was the last time Anderson played the Ghoulardi character in Cleveland, and it happened at Channel 5. Ernie was already doing voice-overs in Los Angeles, and Herman Spero flew him and his wife in for the show. You may recall that Chuck McCann was the guy in the old Right Guard commercial who's on the other side when a guy opens his medicine cabinet. There wasn't much to the show: a few skits that fell flat, a badly butchered version of W. C. Fields's *The Bank Dick*, and some local bands trying to impress Don Webster, who was also on the show. Not the way we expected Ghoulardi to exit, but Ernie really didn't care.

A final note about Ghoulardi: Ernie found out that Storer Broadcasting had copyrighted the name without asking him. As a result he would only signs autographs "Goulardi" without an "h." Chances are, if you have one with an "h" it's a phony.

When Ernie left the late-night job for California in early 1967, WJW started looking for a replacement. They didn't have to look far. Bob Wells had been doing weather, but Dick Goddard's return to Cleveland at Channel 8 pushed him to weekends. Why not have him co-host the Friday night movies with Ghoulardi's old foil, Chuck Schodowski, as *Hoolihan and Big Chuck*? It would take guts to follow a legend like Ernie Anderson, but the two were confident they could pull it off, and so was the station. Assistant general manager Charles Bergerson told the *Cleveland Press* there would be "no taboos." Their audition tape showcased Big Chuck's talent as a straight man along with Hoolihan's flair for satire. Schodowski also made it clear he would continue his job in the control room for two reasons: He had a family to support, and performing in front of the camera scared him to death.

After a time Bob Wells decided to look for other opportunities, and Channel 8 awarded the co-hosting gig to "Lil' John" Rinaldi, who'd been in several skits with Chuck and Hoolihan over the years. The Polish/Italian combination was a perfect fit for Cleveland's heavy ethnic audience. You might recall back in the '60s that Polish jokes were big, and no one laughed louder than people with Polish names. It was "fun to be a Polak!" Chuck had fun with it, too, though in the skits he would refer to the character as a "certain ethnic." It didn't matter. The striped sweater and beat-up fedora were like a uniform. Lil' John remembers doing a "certain ethnic" skit with Chuck on Fleet Avenue, and people beeped and yelled out at John. They didn't notice Chuck, who looked like everyone else on the street! It became the longest running locally produced comedy show in the country. Tom Hanks was a fan when he lived in Cleveland, and the *Wall Street Journal* wrote about Chuck and John on the front page. And a former Clevelander, Carter Bays, paid tribute to the guys in his CBS comedy *How I Met Your Mother*. The episode is titled "Glitter." The lead character, Ted, is from Shaker Heights, and when his old pal Punchy comes to New York for a visit, he bursts in the door, plops down on the couch, and yells out, "Do you get Big Chuck and Lil' John up here?" It meant nothing to anyone outside Cleveland, and that's just the way it was supposed to be.

There were others, most notably Marty Sullivan's "Super Host" on WUAB. He did Saturday afternoons and had a pretty solid audience, but Super Host eventually faded from the airwaves when Sullivan retired.

"... but you can't fool Mom."

Ron Penfound and Captain Penny

CLEVELAND TV HAD ITS stars, and it also had its superstars. Dorothy Fuldheim, Ernie Anderson, Linn Sheldon. They were bigger than life, and Ron Penfound was on that list. He had a beautiful, rich voice, and he knew how to use it. He just didn't end up using it the way he originally intended.

Ron was a local guy, from Elyria. He went to Kenyon College with thoughts about becoming an Episcopal minister, but his roommate got him interested in acting. His name was Paul Newman. That Paul Newman! Ron wanted a little more security, and transferred to the University of Denver to study broadcasting. He got some radio experience in Denver and before long headed back for a couple of radio gigs in Cleveland. In April 1953 he landed a job as a sports announcer at WEWS. Then fate stepped in.

It was no picnic selling TV time. Plenty of homes still didn't have even one set, and advertisers weren't convinced it could sell product. There was a kids' show on the West Coast called *Engineer Bill*, and it was sponsored by Lionel trains. The host dressed as a train engineer, showed cartoons, and sold a lot of trains. *Engineer Bill* also generated a lot of money, and WEWS decided to hop on the train. Betty Cope needed a show to replace Linn Sheldon's *Uncle Leslie*, and on Linn's advice she offered the job to Ron Penfound. It was extra money, though Ron didn't expect it to last. For a short time before he left, Linn Sheldon and Ron Penfound both had shows on WEWS. It came about so quickly that Ron didn't have a name for his show until just before it aired. The name "Penny" from Penfound seems apparent, though Ron's son,

Matt, did some genealogy research and found an Uncle William on his dad's side, who also used the Penny nickname. Whatever the source, on March 2, 1955, we saw the first of Cleveland's own TV train engineer, Captain Penny.

Linn Sheldon was in the control room still dressed as Uncle Leslie. Ron walked into the studio control following the first episode, and Linn said, "Hey, kid, you did a nice job. One little problem: My dad was a railroad man. You've got engineers and porters and brakemen. No captains." Ron looked at Linn, lit a cigarette, and said, "Who cares? This thing's off the air in two weeks." Those two weeks turned into sixteen years.

Ron had a calm, deep, reassuring voice. He moonlighted at a lot of different jobs at the station, from booth announcer to sports and weather reports, but he would always be Captain Penny. The show took off, and Bosco Chocolate Syrup became a major sponsor. There was a special Bosco dispenser with a clown's head on a jar with a removable hat. Within days after it first appeared on *Captain Penny's Fun House*, grocery stores were scrambling to keep up with the demand.

The captain had a cast of regular visitors on the set. When the show had more of a train theme, you had characters such as Mr. Nicklesworth, the porter, who was played by the show's producer, Earl Keyes. Keyes would eventually take over as Mr. Jingeling after the death of Cleveland Playhouse actor Max Ellis. Then there was Professor Yule Flunk, an Irwin Corey-type teacher dressed in a robe and mortar board, played by Jim Breslin. Don't forget Dick Dugan, the *Plain Dealer* cartoonist known as "Doodles," who would sketch out characters on the set.

There were a lot of little life lessons as well. If you listened to Mom and Dad and finished your dinner, they could nominate you for the "Clean Plate Club." To make it a little easier getting through chicken pox, a kid could get a certificate for Captain Penny's "No Scratch Club." When Ron heard that little Prince Charles had come down with the illness, he rushed a certificate off to Buckingham Palace and got a very formal thank-you letter in return. Ratings

Cartoons were a big part of children's programming, and if Captain Penny said they were good you could take it to the bank. Here's a publicity photo of Ron Penfound introducing the new Hanna-Barbera characters, Huckleberry Hound, Yogi Bear, and Quick Draw McGraw. *Cleveland Public Library*

were good, the ad dollars kept rolling in, and Captain Penny was generating a load of money for Channel 5.

When the old *Our Gang* films had been repackaged for syndication as the *Little Rascals,* they found a home on Captain Penny's show, and Channel 5 struck gold again. It cost very little to show the old episodes, and for the baby boomers it was like a whole new series. Captain Penny was turning into "must-see TV" for the whole family! Enter the Three Stooges.

The Stooges' contract with Columbia Pictures had ended in 1959. They filmed 194 shorts over twenty years and were pretty much written out for any residuals from syndication. Columbia turned a quick buck by selling 78 of the films to TV. They were an immediate hit on Captain Penny's show. Ron called them "Tres Patsis," Italian for "Three Stooges," and referred to them as "Larry, Curly, and Moe." Interesting point: In every city but Cleveland they were known as "Moe, Larry, and Curly." The trio were famous for their on-screen pie fights, and Captain Penny even staged a few on his set.

Parents loved the Stooges, too. Well, a lot of parents did. Captain Penny warned kids at the beginning of each show that Larry, Curly, and Moe (and later Shemp and Joe) were to be watched and enjoyed—but never imitated. That didn't really matter. Before long there were reports of kids gouging eyes and conking each other on the head in Cleveland and every city that aired the Stooges.

Channel 5's Don Perris likened the Stooges to a Punch and Judy act. He told the *Press*, "This sort of thing was popular on the Elizabethan stage back in 1640. Why, if the Three Stooges had been performing in 1640 instead of 1940, they would be studied as classical comedians today. The Elizabethan stage had daily performances. There was lots of exposure then, too." It might have been a stretch to think parents would believe the Three Stooges were related in any way to classic British theater.

The controversy revived interest in the Stooges. Steve Allen and Milton Berle had them on their shows, and they went on a tour of nightclubs and theaters with matinees for the kids. They even appeared on Captain Penny and warned kids to laugh at their films but not to try anything like that at home. The complaints still came in, but not as they had when the Stooges first came on the screen.

The Indian Hills PTA in Euclid conducted a survey called "Children Plus Television—Menace or Promise?" Few saw promise. Seventy percent said they had seen "harmful or obnoxious" programming; 25 percent objected to the Three Stooges; and 18 percent had banned them from their TV sets.

The station had to address parents' concerns, and that job went to the general manager, Don Perris. He told the group, "Captain Penny is no mere performer. He is a way of life. He has always tried to teach kids politeness, manners, and respect for mommy."

He also suggested that some of the eye-poking might stem from sibling rivalry. In other words, don't blame us. Some good did come out of all this. The Stooges had a whole new career that might not have happened if they hadn't been cut out of their royalties. They stayed on the road as a team until Larry Fine fell ill and had to go into the old actors' home in L.A. Shows like Captain Penny helped ease him into retirement.

The show had a lot of different theme songs. Those were the days when studio musicians still played live, and Joe Howard and the One O'Clock Club Band came up with *Funny Fun Fun Train*. Keven Scarpino is the "Son of Ghoul," the longest continuing horror show host in the country, and he can still sing the lyrics to this day.

> Here comes Captain Penny with his funny fun fun friends,
>   funny fun fun friends.
> Here comes Captain Penny with his funny fun fun friends,
>   funny fun fun friends.
> Roger Ramjet, Mr. Magoo, Hashimoto, Sydney, and the
>   Astronut, too.
> Here Comes Captain Penny with his funny fun fun friends,
>   funny fun fun friends.
> Here comes Captain Penny with his funny fun fun friends,
>   funny fun fun friends.

That song reflected the cheap syndicated cartoon package Channel 5 had invested in for the show. Cheap cartoons or not, Captain Penny became so popular that he was seen in three different time slots. There was even a Saturday morning show called *Captain Penny's Fun Farm*. He was also seen in prime time, but in a very unlikely role.

Westerns were big in 1961, and Chuck Connors came to Cleveland to plug *The Rifleman*. He was booked for Captain Penny, and he really hit it off with Ron, who mentioned his old roomie, Paul Newman. Connors suggested he come out to L.A. for a role on his show. That's just what Ron did; he was cast as a villain in an

Barbara Plummer was known to the preschool audience as Miss Barbara on *Romper Room* on WEWS. Here, she acceptes flowers to celebrate her seventh year on channel 5. *Cleveland Press Collection, Cleveland State University Archives*

episode titled "The Princess." You can still catch it in reruns, but it has never officially appeared in a *Rifleman* DVD set.

Captain Penny could draw huge crowds. When the new Giant Tiger store opened on Brookpark Road in December 1961, hundreds of kids turned out to see the captain. Even the fire marshal was concerned. The next day marked another celebrity appearance, but that star couldn't compete with Captain Penny when it came to drawing a crowd. That celebrity was Jayne Mansfield.

We mention again that W. C. Fields would tell show biz folks never to work with kids or animals. They steal the show, and you can't trust them. Captain Penny should have thought about that before he went to the Cleveland Zoo with *Romper Room* host Miss Barbara.

Tom Piskura remembered when the station first started using videotape back in 1961. It was a very hot and humid day in August,

Ron Penfound's Captain Penny always kept his cool . . . though
that wasn't easy after this elephant drenched him on a brutally hot
and humid summer day. *Cleveland Public Library*

over 90 degrees, and that was at 9 a.m. The station wanted to get
as much use as they could out of the remote trailer. The plan was to
tape about thirty segments at the zoo, maybe three to five minutes
each, and use them on *Romper Room* and Captain Penny's show.
It was about to become a very long day.

Miss Barbara and Captain Penny were set up near some ele-
phants and were going to interview the trainer. A few seconds
into the interview an elephant vomited through his trunk all
over Captain Penny. None of it got on Miss Barbara, but Ron was
soaked, and it stank to high heaven! Here's the problem: He didn't

have a change of clothes and, as Tom described it, he got fire-hosed by the elephant from head to toe! The captain was not happy!

The show had to go on because the crews had other work scheduled that week and the features had to get on right away. They used a garden hose to get most of whatever it was off of Captain Penny, but the smell was still overpowering. It took most of the day to do those segments, but it seemed a lot longer to everyone who was there. Then there was the monkey, but first let's take a look at the guy who brought it in.

"Jungle Larry" was a regular guest on Captain Penny's show and other shows on the station. He and his wife, "Safari Jane," ran the Zoological Assemblies in Vermilion, and they were often featured on *Mary Ellen's Fun Farm*. They always brought cages filled with exotic animals. One *Fun Farm* show featured Conchita, a giant Brazilian boa constrictor that had given birth to twelve baby snakes the night before and was a little edgy in front of the cameras. Larry and Jane (whose real name was Nancy) could describe the animals in a way that related well to kids. Larry especially seemed to know a lot about animals, but some folks questioned his credentials.

In 1961 KYW ran a locally produced show called *Inquest*. That May it ran an episode titled "Our Image Abroad," and one of the guests was Dr. Lawrence Tetzlaff, the same Jungle Larry over at WEWS. He said he had three postgraduate degrees, including a zoology doctorate from the University of Michigan. Not only that, he claimed that Emperor Haile Selassie had offered him the position of agriculture minister of Ethiopia, which he had politely declined. That had some folks scratching their heads. They decided to check out Larry's credentials.

It turned out that his degrees were a sham. In fact, the University of Michigan told *Press* writer Jim Frankel there was no record of Lawrence Tetzlaff holding any degrees.

When the *Press* confronted Jungle Larry, he said that the records had likely been destroyed in a fire on campus. He would straighten it out when he lectured in Ann Arbor in a few months. That didn't sit well with the university. Evelyn Ward, the university spokesper-

When Jack Hanna was still a pup, Cleveland's "Jungle Larry" Teztlaff was introducing TV audiences to the animals he picked up on his frequent safaris. *Cleveland Public Library*

son, shot back, "Nothing has ever burned here, and we never throw anything away. We have no folder on Mr. Tetzlaff." Jungle Larry wasn't asked back to *Inquest*. Now, about that monkey.

Jungle Larry was still welcome at Channel 5, and on one of his visits he brought along a monkey. It apparently wanted none of this "show-and-tell" stuff and became extremely agitated. In a flash the monkey jumped from Jungle Larry's lap and in one giant leap headed for the studio rafters, where he quickly disappeared into an air conditioning duct. They tried but couldn't find him, though the stench coming out of that duct gave a pretty good clue of what had happened. Jungle Larry was no longer permitted to bring in monkeys for show and tell.

Murphy's Law was in full swing when Jungle Larry came by.

Anything could happen and usually did. One day he brought a trio of snakes, the "Three Musketeers," and convinced Ron Penfound he should wrestle one. Plus, Larry wasn't always the animal's friend. A boa constrictor once wrapped itself tightly around him while he and the snake were taking a shower. Fortunately, he had the presence of mind to stand still while an assistant removed it. Another time a cheetah attacked him on live TV while he was trying to get him out of a cage. Captain Penny often looked a little nervous when Larry paid a visit.

As local kids' shows went by the wayside, Captain Penny hung on longer than most. He updated his image over the years, putting on a blazer instead of a train outfit, but the show came to an end on September 4, 1971. Ron was still getting work at WEWS as a weekend weatherman and staff announcer, and he worked as many Indians games as he could at Municipal Stadium. Even so, he thought it was time to leave, and that's just what he did in 1972. His first stop was New Hampshire and then Naples, Florida, near his old friend Jungle Larry. It should also be pointed out that Jungle Larry remained a devoted friend to the Penfounds long after Ron's death. A little over three years after his final farewell as Captain Penny, Ron Penfound passed away on September 16, 1974.

We all have our special memories of Captain Penny, but perhaps the most eloquent tribute came from his son, Matt. In a speech honoring his dad at a broadcasters' dinner, Matt said:

"I suppose some might feel slighted having to share their father with thousands of other children, but somehow when I bump into a forty-five-year-old 'kid' and they tell me how much my father meant to them, it doesn't seem like such a bad thing.

"Professionally, my dad had an amazing career, but it's the other things about him that I remember the most. He loved racing, and he loved baseball. I only wish he had known the Indians of the 1990s instead the 1960s. I'll always remember how much he loved his parents, how he respected them. How much he loved my mom, Jodie Penfound. I also remember how my dad faced the end of his life with strength and dignity.

This friendly train conductor thought the show would only be on for a couple of weeks. Captain Penny was on Cleveland TV for 16 years. *Cleveland Public Library*

"There were those little lessons about life that he taught my sisters and myself [*sic*]. Like respecting other people, especially older adults. It's no surprise that his favorite radio and television personality was a woman by the name of Dorothy Fuldheim. His favorite football player was George Blanda, not because he was that great but because he was forty-seven years old, and he was still playing football. My dad said that older adults needed to be respected and admired and looked up to, and I always remembered that.

"He also taught me not to wait for life to give you what you think you deserve, and I'm still learning that lesson. I can still hear him. If I said, 'Dad, I wish I had this,' he would say, 'You know, Son, if wishes were horses, beggars would ride.' That was his way of saying, 'Don't beg for it. Don't just sit around and wish for it. Go out and make it happen.'

"He also said, and I think Benjamin Franklin first said it, 'God helps those who help themselves.' He was the son of an Elyria steel worker, and Dad did just that, and in the process he touched thousands of lives.

"Charles Kingsley said that when we go to bed at night we should be able to say, 'I made at least one person today a little wiser, a little happier, or a little better.' I believe that my dad and the others we honor posthumously tonight were able to say just that. Maybe when we remember them, rather than just remembering, maybe our smile and our attitude will also help to make a difference."

Ron's memory lives on, and so do his words. At the end of every show he would give the kids at home advice adapted from both Abraham Lincoln and *The Little Rascals'* Spanky McFarland:

"You can fool some of the people all of the time, and all of the people some of the time, but you can't fool Mom. She's pretty nice and pretty smart—you listen to her and you won't go far wrong."

The Man Behind Mr. Magoo

Jim Backus

ODDLY ENOUGH, ONE OF the most recognized voices in children's television never did any real time on Cleveland TV, but he had a definite link to Northeast Ohio. We all know the voice of "Mr. Magoo," the nearsighted cartoon character who would end every adventure with, "Oh Magoo! You've done it again!" He was a long-time favorite on NBC, but people knew Jim Backus's voice before his face.

Backus grew up in Bratenahl and went to University School. He got the acting bug by reading a kids' magazine, *Captain Billy's Whiz Bang*, in his attic. He would act the stories out by reading them aloud, and he started doing voices for each character. That led to summer stock theater, and it paid off big. In the early 1940s he became the youngest staff announcer in America when he landed the job at WTAM, and that's where he met up with Tom Lewis. They didn't work there together long. Lewis got canned, and when Backus told his dad he would probably be next, he got some unlikely advice. His father said, "Don't let them get at you! You go in tomorrow morning and quit! Don't let them get the jump on you." Backus did just that . . . and found himself in the same boat as Tom Lewis. Unemployed.

Backus and Lewis decided to head straight to the top. They gathered up all their savings and jumped into a rattletrap car. "New York City. Here we come!" Problem was, neither had a sense of direction or could read a map. They left Cleveland and thought they were making pretty good time until they ended up in Ashtabula . . . eight hours later! Even so, there were some good things on the horizon.

The two finally made it to New York, and those hours practicing in the attic paid off for Backus. He knocked on a few doors and got picked up as a voice actor for network radio shows. He developed a character named Hubert Updyke III with a refined New England accent similar to the one he used in his role years later on *Gilligan's Island.* It was actually based on a neighbor who lived across the street in Bratenahl. Danny Kaye and Alan Young had Updyke III on their shows, and he was a big hit. The character turned out to be his ticket to Hollywood and lots of work in movies.

When he first made it to Tinsel Town, Backus had to find a place to live fast. He ended up renting an apartment from Eva Gabor before her star started to rise. Backus didn't see a radiator, and still wary of what winter was like back in Cleveland, asked, "Where does the heat come from?" Eva shot back, "We don't need a furnace here! We have a big pot of Hungarian goulash simmering all day. That throws off a lot of heat." In later years when Backus was a panelist on the *What's My Line?* quiz show, Gabor came on as a mystery guest. When the panelists removed their masks, Backus yelled out, "My landlady!" Eva called back, "Dolling! How do you like sleeping in my bed!?" Backus was quick to explain what she meant, but not before there were some anxious moments for the folks in the control room.

TV was just getting off the ground in the early '50s, and Backus was there from the start. He played a judge on *I Married Joan* and did lots of commercial voice work. The party circuit loved him, too, especially when he knocked a few back and started doing "Magoo." It was a character voice he had created for a 1949 film titled *Ragtime Bear.* It was at one of those parties where a TV producer saw him, and the nearsighted legend was born.

At first Backus didn't want to do Mr. Magoo. He had every intention of being a Shakespearean actor . . . until the checks started rolling in. He said his thoughts about the Bard disappeared every time he went to the bank. Backus moved to Bel Air and built a house with a basement and furnace, which even now is a rarity in Southern California. The voice opened doors outside of TV, too.

Long before Thurston Howell III landed on *Gilligan's Island*, Cleve-lander Jim Backus was known as the voice of the myopic cartoon character Mr. Magoo. *Cleveland Public Library*

In January 1963 Backus wanted to treat eight of his friends to a spa in Long Beach. He called for a dinner reservation at a swanky restaurant and was told the earliest he could possibly get in was May, four months later. That didn't sit well with Jim Backus. He called back as Mr. Magoo and not only got the time he wanted that Saturday night but Cary Grant's table, to boot!

Magoo's fans were legion, and Backus continued to do specials. The older fans remembered his face from *I Married Joan,*" but in 1963 a call from an old friend would introduce him to a whole new audience. Sherwood Schwartz wrote the lines for Backus when he played Hubert Updyke, and he wanted to revive the character with a different name on his new TV series, *Gilligan's Island.* Backus had his doubts. There were good and bad points about a weekly series. He likened it to watching your mother-in-law drive over a cliff in your new Cadillac. But Gilligan struck a chord, and Backus became as rich as the character he played, Thurston Howell III. So rich that he claimed to have two Cadillacs in his garage, one for right turns and one for left. One more point: *Gilligan's Island* had another connection to Northeast Ohio. The late Russell Johnson played "Professor" Roy Hinkley, a high school science teacher from Cleveland, Ohio.

Santa's Man in Cleveland

Mr. Jingeling Brings Christmas to the Small Screen

TELEVISION TOOK THE CHRISTMAS season to an entirely new level. Commercials became as important as programming because kids could now see toys in action before they started bugging their parents. Some of the ads, like Remco's "Whirlybird" helicopter, were somewhat deceiving. They showed the copter flying on its own when in reality it had two slow-moving propellers. The company changed the ad after a wave of complaints from both parents and kids.

Through the 1950s and early '60s, downtown Cleveland was the epicenter for Christmas shopping. Shopping malls were few and far between, and trolleys, buses, and rapid transit trains were packed heading into town. During the annual Cleveland Christmas parade, the streets of downtown looked more like Manhattan, and families who came out stayed to shop. Department stores had huge mechanical displays to lure in the shoppers, but TV gave them an opportunity to reach out to folks in the suburbs. One store in particular needed a spokesman, and a TV legend was born.

In December 1956 WEWS introduced Mr. Jingeling to its TV audience. He was created by Frank Jacobi at the Chicago ad agency that handled the Halle's Department Store account. Jingeling was one of Santa's helpers who had created a key to unlock the Treasure House of Toys and save Christmas. There was even a record telling how he came to be the "keeper of the keys." He set up shop locally on Halle's seventh floor, and thousands of kids came out the first year to see him up close and walk away with a souvenir paper key. (You pay a lot for those keys now on eBay!) What was supposed to have been a one-shot promotion became an annual holiday tradition.

Jingeling became such a hit that Halle's even had some of its delivery drivers dress like him on their runs. No one complained, either. What delivery man got that kind of reception when he walked up a driveway?

The other stores knew Halle's was onto something. Every one of them had a Santa Claus, but Jingeling had TV time, and that drew in a lot of people. Higbee's department store tried to counter with a couple of characters named "Higg" and "Bee." They were played by two kid actors, eight-year-old Johnny Burton and nine-year-old Gail Petziner. Henry Alexander, the advertising manager for Higbee's, convinced WEWS to air the segments even though it already had Mr. Jingeling. Gail had some show biz experience. She was one of the finalists for the local *Mickey Mouse Club Show* Talent Hunt, and her buck teeth and freckles were the look Higbee's wanted. She also knew Johnny from Sunday school, so they had some on-air chemistry. They talked with kids from other countries about their holiday traditions and sang Christmas carols, but the segment never really took off. Jingeling was the big dog on the block.

The Mr. Jingeling segments were glorified commercials. They usually involved Jingeling getting into some type of a jam, and that day's toy came to the rescue. Even so, kids didn't see the connection, and if you saw Mr. Jingeling in person you watched him on TV, too. The segments ran for about five minutes twice a day during the Captain Penny shows at 12:40 and 6:45 p.m., with a full half-hour special just before Christmas. In the beginning there were two Mr. Jingelings. Tom Moviel, a Cleveland cop who was also a local actor, played Jingeling at the store, but the TV job was a union gig. Tom had a houseful of kids and didn't want to put out the cash for the initiation fee and dues. The TV role went to Max Ellis, an actor from the Cleveland Playhouse who originally had played Santa Claus on Channel 5. Eventually Ellis took over the role full time.

It didn't take long for Jingeling to become a superstar. By

"How you ting-e-ling!" Max Ellis was a renowned actor at the Cleveland Playhouse when he got the nod to be Mr. Jingeling in the 1950s. *Cleveland Press Collection, Cleveland State University Archives*

November 1958 he was kicking off the Christmas season with a *Toy Land* TV special along with another kid's show actor, "Joe the Cloud" Berg. Bill Prentice, a booth announcer at WEWS, got the role of Santa Claus because he could belt out "Ho, ho, ho!" better than anyone else on the staff. When Jingeling and Santa ended their run that year, Prentice told the *Cleveland Press*, "During the three weeks we've been on the air we've received forty-thousand applications from kiddies who want to talk to Santa. However, we can only invite twenty-five a day to come down to the studio. Of the twenty-five, only four get before the cameras. But after each telecast I take each child aside and ask him what he wants for Christmas." It would appear the kids were aware of world and national news at that time. Prentice said boys especially were opting for toys such as rockets and satellite launchers, while girls, who were

A TV Christmas tradition. Pat Dopp, The Story Lady, trades tales with Max Ellis as Mr. Jingeling on his segments that ran during the holiday season on Captain Penny's show. *Cleveland Press, author's collection*

just as aware of the world situation, still wanted traditional toys like dolls. He also said that one kid wanted handcuffs so he could rob a bank by restraining a guard. Prentice got some very weird answers when he asked kids what they wanted to be when they grew up. One girl said she wanted to be a man. It's anyone's guess whether she succeeded.

By 1960 Jingeling was so busy that Santa himself would appear on the Captain Penny show. In reality the Santa segments were sponsored by Kresge's Department Stores and couldn't be connected to Higbee's. He would bring along a puppet, "Twinkie, the Elf," who was voiced by Mary Jo Perkins, the wife of newsman Jack Perkins before he went national on NBC.

Max Ellis played Mr. Jingeling into the early '60s, but died of a heart attack in the summer of 1964. Like Linn Sheldon, Ellis had had a long career on local stages. He performed more than two

Mr. Jingeling—The Next Generation. Earl Keyes was last in a line of TV's "Keeper of the Keys." He held that title longer than anyone else and, ironically, died the day after Christmas in 2000. *Cleveland Press Collection, Cleveland State University Archives*

hundred roles at the Cleveland Play House and did radio as well, but he was best known as Mr. Jingeling. The new Mr. Jingeling was Carl Mackey. He had a long history as managing director at the Lakewood Little Theater, and he took over the Jingeling role, but only for one season. By 1965 Halle's had a "Help Wanted" sign on its seventh floor. Earl Keyes made his move.

Earl had a long history at WEWS, not only as a producer but playing roles as well. He was probably best known as "Mr. Nickelsworth," the train porter on Captain Penny's show. Plus, he knew the Jingeling character from producing the segments for Max Ellis and Carl Mackey. It seemed like a no-brainer. Earl took the job in 1965 and brought some extra help. His wife, Nadine, would occasionally play the role of Mrs. Jingeling. Things would change just a few years later.

As popular as he was, Mr. Jingeling got a pink slip in 1969 from Halle's and WEWS when the store pulled its sponsorship. Earl stayed on at Channel 5 playing Santa, but Mr. Jingeling would be on an extended vacation until 1974. That's when he found a new home at WUAB. Earl was back in the saddle. He told an interviewer that grateful parents would often "have a snort ready for Jingy" when he delivered presents to children's homes. (That obviously never happened. Jingeling didn't make house calls.) He also admitted the tufts of hair on his head frightened some kids, who thought they resembled horns.

Most of us of a certain age have trouble remembering what we had for breakfast, but we can still sing Mr. Jingeling's theme song:

Mister Jingeling! How you tingeling! Keeper of the keys.
On Halle's Seventh Floor we'll be looking for you to turn the
    keys.
He keeps track of Santa's sack and treasure house of toys,
With wind-up things that Santa brings to all the little girls
    and boys.

And for those with really keen memories, there was also a variation:

Mr. Jingeling! How you tingeling! Keeper of the keys.
Don't you dare be late for we have a date on Halle's Seventh
    Floor.

"My dad wants to sell you a car now!"

Commercials

COMMERCIALS HAVE ALWAYS BEEN the lifeblood of broadcasting, but they were a different animal on TV. You needed visuals, and photos just didn't hold the viewer's interest. That opened the door for some very creative people to make the ad man's ideas come to life. There was big money in beer. Most early TVs were set up in taverns, so beer had a solid audience. John Fitzgerald worked in a brewery before he started as a sportscaster at WXEL, which became WJW. His *Sports Final* show was sponsored by Carling Black Label beer, and John would end his segment with a whistle and the slogan, "Hey Mabel! Black Label!" The company liked it so much they made it part of their national advertising campaign.

P.O.C. had spots with whomever was the TV host raising a glass with the "Pride of Cleveland." It actually stood for "Pilsener on Call" or, if you didn't like it, "Piss on Cleveland." Then there was Duquesne, or "Duke" for short. That company sponsored Dorothy Fuldheim's commentaries in the '50s, and she would sit behind the logo on the front of her desk with the "prince of pilsener" holding a glass of beer right below. Carling Brewing Co. actually put some money into crude animation with a spot that changed as many as twenty slides in forty seconds, far faster than could be changed by hand. The live spots were still the most economical, and often the most tricky. Linn Sheldon had a show sponsored by Standard Brewing. The beer was Erin Brew, and the media buyer wanted to show how much of a head it had when you poured it into the glass. Linn hid a case in the station's freezer so the camera crew wouldn't find it, and he brought it out when it was time to plug the sponsor. The problem was, there was no head. No beer! He popped the cap with a church key, and it was frozen solid. Chances are the audience took his word that Erin was a pretty good beer.

Another company named Standard (Standard Oil) dropped a lot of money into television. It sponsored Warren Guthrie's newscasts, but the real audience came during the Indians games. The company wanted something to pop out of the screen, so they hired Jasper Wood (who won three May Show art competitions in the '40s and early '50s) to design a 20-by-40 foot background. Then the director at WEWS, Jim Breslin, would move a cut-out of "Boris Boron" driving along while a booth announcer read the spot. Crude, but effective.

Not all the car ads went over as well. WKBF aired a spot in 1968 that showed Cleveland Browns great Lou Groza kicking out windshields to plug a Bedford Auto Mile dealer. People called the station to complain, offended by the wanton destruction. The station substituted an ad showing Groza kicking a field goal.

The kids' programs moved a lot of product, too. Mickey's Jim Jams and Banana Flips, prize eggs from Red Goose Shoes, fast food, cereals, and gallons upon gallons of Bosco flew off the shelves if Captain Penny or Barnaby gave them the thumbs up. And the stores had slogans that stay with us today. "Uncle Bill's is for the people!" "Every day is savings day on everything at Revco." A & P had, "We won't stop trying 'til you say WEO!" (which stood for Warehouse Economy Outlet) and "The biggest mall in all the world is Randall Park!"

Jingles were a big draw, too. Soft drinks were well represented, and Cotton Club led the way. "Hey, Big Ginger," "Come on over," and "There's absolutely positively without a doubt no sugar in sugar-free Cotton Club." We all remember "School bells ring and children sing. It's back to Robert Hall again." "Half the fun of having feet is Red Goose Shoes." (Honk!) And the story of "The Big O," how one man slept while the other man drove the "cold, cold juice in the tank truck caboose" to get fresh o.j. to Lawson's in forty hours. Talk about driving. "Chevy, Chevy. See Commander Ray, at West Park Chevrolet," and Del Spitzer's "My dad wants to sell you a car now!" Don't forget the owners. Ed Stinn filled the screen, and you could "See the USA in a C. Miller Chevrolet!" with a big, wet kiss thrown at you. You might have never met "that Marolis," but the jingle promised he was a great, great guy because he could "save you money on that Chevy buy!" And, course, there was the schmaltzy but lingering melody, "It's a beautiful thing you got at the showcase of beautiful cars, Hal Artz." The commercials and jingles stayed with us long after the people who had made them went on to their "greater reward."

He Was Made for Children's Television

Woodrow, the Woodsman

ONE PERFORMER ON CLEVELAND TV was always pretty much in Linn Sheldon's shadow, and he didn't mind that one bit. His name was J. Clayton Conroy, who had a series of jobs before he landed in television. Clay was a magician, a trombone player, and could swim like a fish. He even performed in the water show at Cypress Gardens in Florida. His wife was from the Cleveland area and wanted to move back, so they headed north, and Clay started looking for work. He'd done some theater, and in 1961 he heard about a possible opening at KYW-TV. Linn Sheldon couldn't keep up with the demand for Barnaby's personal appearances and needed help on and off the screen. Linn recalled a long line at the auditions and even remembered Dick Goddard in the crowd. Then it was Clay's turn.

Linn said it was a perfect fit right from the start. Years later he said, "We anticipated each other's moves and could improvise and ad lib and still know where the bit was heading." They decided the new character would be a woodsman, "Woodrow, the Woodsman," and he was introduced on Barnaby's Saturday morning show. Sadly, no tapes exist, but the story line was a series of weird things happening and Barnaby and Woodrow missing each other by seconds. When they finally stumbled upon each other, Woodrow introduced himself, saying, "I've lived in forests all over the world, but I finally decided to settle down in the Enchanted Forest." He settled in for a long stay. It wasn't long before Woodrow was as busy as the guy he was hired to help. He got his own show every

Clay Conroy's Woodrow, the Woodsman was so popular that he was brought back to Cleveland TV in the 1990s. It got plenty of his old fans, now parents themselves, out of bed on Saturday mornings to relive the good old days. *Cleveland Press Collection, Cleveland State University Archives*

Clay Conroy as Woodrow and Linn Sheldon as Barnaby. These two kids' show hosts worked so well together they could anticipate each other's every move. *Cleveland Press Collection, Cleveland State University Archives*

day at 4:30, and it was a big hit, with a cast of talking animals to keep it moving. There was "Tarkington Whom III the Owl," who spoke with a sophisticated British accent. "Frederick Maximilian Gesundheit (Freddie) the Ali-croc" had a German accent and an edgy sense of humor, and "Voracious the Elephant" had a huge appetite for peanut butter sandwiches. The voices were done by Lawson Deming, who also worked the puppets. Woodrow was a top draw, and Clay Conroy couldn't have been happier.

Northeast Ohio had a reputation as one of the most charitable regions in the country, and that extended all the way to kids. In the early '60s you had Ghoulardi, Miss Barbara, Captain Penny, Barnaby, Woodrow, and Franz the Toymaker pushing everything from UNICEF to the United Appeal's "Red Feather," and they all brought in big money. Woodrow, Captain Penny, and especially Barnaby promoted backyard carnivals for the Muscular Dystrophy Association. They were neighborhood events that brought in money a penny at a time and raised more than $10,000 in the first year alone. Part of that success was through personal appearances, and Clay as Woodrow tried to show up for every invitation. Very few of those muscular dystrophy carnival kits survived the '60s and command big prices when they pop up on eBay.

Barnaby and Woodrow were a one-two ratings punch! Holidays were especially busy, and the 1964 special *Three Nights Before Christmas* brought in a huge audience. That special was memorable for a number of reasons, including Dick Goddard's singing debut with "White Christmas." It was also an opportunity to see Barnaby and Woodrow in prime time. KYW scheduled Clay's show, *Woodrow's Zoo Parade*, at 12:30 p.m. on Saturdays and on Mondays at 1 a.m. after *The Tonight Show*! Right to the end he could never explain that time slot.

By December 1965 the ad dollar started to dictate what went on the air, and Woodrow was moved exclusively to weekends. The show was number one in its time slot, but GM Neil Van Ells pulled the trigger, saying "The station gets a better dollar return on a daily syndicated strip than on a locally produced children's show." Blunt and to the point! About ten months later Woodrow was cancelled, and Clay and Lawson Deming were shown the door. But there was a bright light at the end of the tunnel. Just a few days later, WJBK-TV in Detroit offered both of them a daily and Saturday "Woodrow" slot. Plus, Deming got additional work playing the horror host, Sir Graves Ghastly, for the next fifteen years! He was as big in Detroit as Ghoulardi was in Cleveland.

(By the way . . . a few years after Deming passed away in 2007, his producer from Detroit traveled to Cleveland to meet Lawson's son David. He was amazed by the resemblance and offered David a chance to bring Graves Ghastly back to the screen. David had to turn him down. Over the years he'd gained a reputation as a world-class sculptor, which meant long hours in the studio. David was also the president of the Cleveland Institute of Art, so he just didn't have the time. Graves Ghastly would have to remain a cherished memory.)

Clay Conroy came back to Cleveland in 1971 to film *We're Young*, a special about the city's 175th birthday. It got a great response, and the next year WKYC gave him a shot at a new series called *Hey Woody!*, which had a format similar to *Laugh-In*. Lawson Deming came down from Detroit to help him out, but the pilot show didn't get picked up. Woodrow was forced to hang up his axe in March 1972, but that's not the end of his story.

Clay still did plenty of commercials and voice-over work, and even got a role in the sequel to the movie *A Christmas Story*, titled *A Summer Story*. Things changed in 1997, when TV producer Dave Little and his lifelong friend Tom Grove came into the picture.

As Dave recalls, "In early 1997, I had been contacted by GM Rich O'Dell at WKYC TV-3 to dub an old Quad tape of a Woodrow show over to VHS tape. Once that was done, I got Clay's address from Big Chuck and called Clay to see if he might want a copy for himself. He did, so I delivered it personally to his Lyndhurst home. While there, he showed me his basement museum of Woodrow artifacts and puppets. Everything was there except the original set, and he had several photographs of that, too. It was during that visit that he complained bitterly about how he and Linn had been unfairly canceled at KYW in the '60s. He also seemed open to going back on the air if the opportunity ever presented itself."

Now keep in mind that that this was the 1990s and, nostalgia aside, there would be some questions about whether an old kids' show could be resurrected and have the same success. Dave promised him nothing at the time, but the wheels were turning in his head. He also seemed pretty confident. "After all, I was working at Image Video Teleproduction, so I had a TV production studio at my disposal, and since I had been producing TV commercials for local TV advertisers there, I had a list of potential advertisers to whom I could pitch the show. That old Quad tape had begun the process of returning Woodrow to the Cleveland airways." But revenue is still the lifeblood of TV programming, and Dave was able to get a sponsor in short order. "That was the result of having Fleming Foods/IGA as a production client at Image. In March 1997, I pitched the show to the baby boomer advertising staff at Fleming Foods, who were also Woodrow fans from the '60s. They quickly grasped the fact that even though Woodrow would air as a kids' show, it would command a serious number of forty-year-old-plus old-time Woodrow viewers (now parents), who would gladly shop at their local IGA stores. But to seal the deal with Fleming, I had to get it on the air. So I built the set and shot the pilot (both at my cost). With a finished pilot in hand, I then pitched the show to three Cleveland TV stations on the same day in April 1997." Clay slipped right back into character, and Tom Grove took over Lawson Deming's role. But now the show needed a station to call home.

"First was Rich O'Dell at WKYC TV-3 who started all of this. O'Dell wanted the show, but only as a one-time special tied to their fiftieth anniversary, not as a weekly series. The second station was WEWS TV-5, who delayed a decision until key personnel returned; and WJW Fox-8.

"Within minutes of screening the pilot, GM Kevin Salyer picked us up for a weekly Saturday morning series beginning that September 1997. For the next three years we never looked back. Fleming Foods/IGA was our only sponsor, and Fox-8 was our only outlet. It was a marriage made in heaven until Clay's health and the one-hour drive to Image became an issue."

Dave says Clay jumped at the chance. "I think he felt redemption, and that with the show back on the air, he would have the last word. Take THAT, Van Ells!!"

From the very first show it was obvious that the Woodrow we knew and loved as kids was back, and so were his puppets. It was as though he had never left. There were guest stars, too. Big Chuck and Lil' John, Dick Goddard, Bob "Hoolihan" Wells, Art Lofredo, Big Stash, and even Soupy Sales. Some of the funniest bits came when Clay was oblivious to the humor in comments not meant to be understood by kids. For example, Sales mentioned Woodrow had a boat. "Why, I don't have a boat," to which Soupy responded, "Really? All the ladies say you have a little dinghy!" Even the puppets would get in a line or two. When Woodrow was anticipating a trip abroad, Freddie stressed he would have to get a complete physical. Woodrow said, "I love going to the doctor!" Freddie looked at the camera and let out a chuckle, like, *Boy! Are you in for a surprise!*

The program was taped at Image Video in Canton, and while every show that aired was seamless, there was an occasional bump off-screen. One day Clay got into his costume, pulled on his tights, and pulled Dave over to say, "We can't tape this week. I forgot my athletic supporter." Sure enough. He couldn't go on camera with those skin-tight pants. It looked like he was smuggling grapes! Luckily there was a store nearby, and Tom Grove drove Clay over to buy a new cup . . . at Dick's Sporting Goods.

Sadly, we missed out on opportunities to see Woodrow's final performances, though in at least one case there was a silver lining. With Clay starting to feel his age, plans were drawn to bring the Woodrow show to an end. In January 2000, Clay informed Fox-8 that the show would not be returning for the 2000–2001 season.

Everyone behind the show knew it eventually would have to end. In fact, Dave recalls, "The decision to create a final show was discussed within weeks of the beginning. We knew we had to end the show someday, and we wanted it to be well thought out. But when it came time to end the show, we all agreed on a plan to keep it going. Even Kevin Salyer liked the plan." You might be surprised by Clay's replacements. It was decided the new hosts would be Big Chuck and Lil' John. "Having been on the show multiple times, they happily agreed to take over the show. But this time they would be park rangers who would protect the Enchanted Forest and feed the animals. Chuck even came up with the show's new name. It was to be called *The Lonely Rangers*." But there had to be a smooth transition, something memorable, and that meant the return of another legend.

The production crew came up with a story line. Dave remembers it this way: "Woodrow was going out on the road as a professional musician, and Linn Sheldon (Barnaby), his agent/manager, would be stopping by to help him pack. He told the animals that he (Woodrow) would return from time to time (cameo appearances), and that they would be well cared for in the interim. Our ultimate plan was to have Woodrow and Barnaby walk into the sunset together as the final scene of the final show (under credits)." The puppets would remain as characters in the new show, and the crew even started taping the final episode. The first segment set up Woodrow's departure, telling the animals he wanted to follow his lifelong dream to be a traveling musician, though Freddie was sarcastically reluctant to believe he would ever leave.

Dave says the second segment was taped with some legendary names. He says, "It was shot at Cuyahoga Community College with Woodrow actually on stage (during rehearsal), playing trombone with the real Four Freshmen band, therefore proving to everyone that he was in fact a professional musician ready for the road. The Four Freshmen had booked Image to record their live Tri-C concert performance for a DVD." Clay had a great time on stage with the guys, who seemed to enjoy it just as much. The surviving footage shows a classic kids' show host doing what he did best in a very funny and poignant scene: setting up his final farewell. The problem was, that scene would never be filmed.

Author's Note: Dave Little and I made several attempts to convince Linn to do that episode. He would never commit to a date. In fact, Dave even promised him a limo, dinner, and of course a modest *per diem*. No dice. It would have been the last show of 2000. There had also been plans—more like a fervent hope—to get

Clay Conroy and Linn Sheldon together for a final appearance. To see Clay and Linn together again would have been a baby boomer's dream come true. So why didn't it happen? They obviously respected each other and knew how important that meeting would have been. Well, a couple of reasons come to mind. One, over a long career. Linn had done a lot more than Barnaby, but that was all people seemed to want to talk about. But there was another reason. I would often ask Linn why he didn't talk about Clay, or why he didn't want to do any TV appearances with him. He would just shrug it off until one day he finally filled me in.

"He's got my Lyle Ritz record!"

What? Who's Lyle Ritz? It turns out that Lyle Ritz played bass for a famed group of studio musicians called the Hollywood Wrecking Crew. They played on everything: Sinatra, the Beach Boys, the Association, Linda Ronstadt . . . you name it, they backed them up. The only thing the acts would supply were vocals. Members of the Crew had hundreds of gold records but none in their own name. They were hired hands and made a lot of money doing it. Now, the interesting thing about Lyle Ritz is that he was from Cleveland and headed to the West Coast to do studio work. That came as a surprise to Linn. Plus, at the time he had only put out one record under his own name, and that was ukulele music. It was titled "How About Uke?" Linn, who could more than hold his own on ukulele, thought Lyle Ritz was the best. That was high praise. "So why don't you just buy another copy?" Turned out the album was out of print and was never relased on compact disc. The wheels started to turn.

I called Clay's number and asked if he had a Lyle Ritz record. Sure enough, he did. He didn't hesitate. "Yeah, you can borrow it. Come on over." When I went to his house, he handed me the copy of "How About Uke?" with "Property of Clay Conroy" stamped all over the back. As I left, I thanked Clay for trusting me with the LP. "Oh, I don't trust you. Just bring it back!"

I was working at a radio station at the time, and the production director copied it to CD. I even copied and shrank the cover so it fit inside the jewel case. I went over to Winton Place condos, knocked on Linn's door, and gave him the copy. His eyes opened wide. "I want to check something," he said. The original vinyl copy had worn over the years, and this was a straight dub. Linn put it in the CD player and went to track number three. "This sounds like my copy. I'll be able to tell because there should be loud click . . ." POP! Right on cue! "Right there! I accidentally dropped my needle on it. That's from my copy." He called me later that night to say that he and his wife, Laura, had laughed and danced and had a great time listening to the CD. Oh, and I returned the record to Clay, but it didn't end there.

Linn was doing book signings for his book, *Barnaby and Me*, and was set up outside the Borders store at La Place in Beachwood. There was the usual long line, and who should come walking through but Clay and his wife, Margie. Clay and Linn's eyes locked. Linn stood up and loudly stated, "Ladies and gentlemen, there is my good friend Clay Conroy!" He insisted that Clay join him and sign books! Clay was as surprised as anyone, and if you got one of the rare copies with both signatures you are extremely fortunate. They went out to dinner with their wives, and the hatchet was officially buried.

Dave Little stayed in touch with Clay the way I did with Linn. Dave and I had known each other for many years and often talked about getting these two great performers together again for a Christmas special. We would film at Stan Hywet Hall, and it would center on Linn and Clay enjoying an old-fashioned Christmas. Carolers would knock on the door, and they would be Woodrow's puppets along with our wives, Laura Sheldon, Margie Conroy, Connie Little, and Janice Olszewski. Another scene would have the two watching Mr. Jingeling on TV and remembering past Christmases. "The toy train around the tree!" Suddenly, Ron Penfound's son, Matt, would magically appear, maybe in the train conductor's outfit! "My dad could tell you about trains." One might say, "And all the toys piled up on Christmas morning." Franz the Toymaker: "Did you say toys?" "Oh, and the kids! The looks on their faces!"

Miss Barbara appears, puts down her magic mirror that she used to see children at home, and say, "I know all about kids!" It would have been a chance to remember all the favorite kids' show hosts. There was still a little bit of a problem . . .

Linn said, "No! Not Barbara Plummer!" Now what? "We both grew up in Norwalk, but I'm a little older than her. Her dad was a doctor there. I babysat her once!"

And? Linn looked embarrassed. "She was getting toilet-trained! I had to put her on the potty!" They were still good friends, and I mentioned to Linn that they were both in their seventies. I didn't think she remembered. "Oh, she remembers! She laughs about it!" It took some time, but I finally convinced Linn in a phone call that he should do the special. The final scene would have been just him and Clay saying goodbye. When he gave me the okay, I called Dave right away, and we started planning. The phone rang again just a few seconds after I hung up. It was Linn. He said Clay was too ill to do it. Clay died a few months later. A couple of months after that I mentioned to Linn that it would have been the most famous special ever on Cleveland TV, one they would have played for many years. He just looked at me, gave a sad smile, and said, "I know."

Broadcasting can be likened to a meat grinder. It consumes the people who devote their lives to it, uses what it can, and discards them when they are of no further use. Very few people, especially nowadays, can say they retired from broadcasting. Most are carried out on their shield, but Clay Conroy fought the broadcast wars and was able to leave on his own terms with his head held high. In the end, thanks to some guardian angels, Clay left a winner.

The Battle Behind the Glass

Sports on TV

THE FOLKS WHO PUT TV on the air in Cleveland needed viewers fast if they wanted to survive. Fortunately, Cleveland's sports teams in the late '40s were red hot, and that's what drew the audience to the tube. Even so, there were some moments in sports that might have been better left off the screen.

Football was a different game in the early '50s. The equipment was poor, rules were different. and as was so often the case, anything could happen. The worst happened to Browns' quarterback Otto Graham in November 1953. Helmets were different then, and his face was pretty much wide open. Graham took a flying elbow into the face that led to fifteen stitches, and then he went back into the game! Problem was, he also had a weekly show on WEWS where he would talk about what had happened on the field. Graham didn't have to talk about the injury. That week the stitches spoke for themselves. He told the *Cleveland Press*, "I don't want anybody to get the idea that I'm a corny exhibitionist. I'm simply going ahead with the show because I feel well enough to appear on it. I had a good night's sleep and my mouth hardly hurts at all." It was still pretty evident that he had taken a real beating on the field.

When Art Modell took over the team he kept a close eye on his broadcast team. If he didn't like you, you were history. That happened to Gib Shanley for one game. Gib and Art were friends and stayed that way their whole lives. The Browns were getting pummeled during one game in 1963, and at halftime Gib made the off-hand remark as they headed to the locker room, "This is the first time the Browns have crossed midfield all day!" Art Modell flipped and ordered Shanley off the broadcast team. Public outcry

"I got your flag right here!" Gib Shanely made colleagues at WEWS very nervous when he lit an Iranian flag on fire live on the air during the 11 p.m. newscast on November 8, 1979—amid the Iranian hostage crisis.

brought him back, and Gib remained one of Art's biggest support-ers even after he moved the Browns to Baltimore.

More about Shanley. He was one of the most well-respected radio and TV voices in the country, but he was seen in a whole new light when Channel 5 went color. That's because his ghastly taste in sport jackets would draw immediate attention even if you didn't care about the home teams. He made a lot of money during his career, becoming the first sportscaster to earn more than $100,000. But when he started calling the Browns games in 1961, he was driving a Fiat with a door that had to be wired shut.

Then there was the Indians. They won the World Series in 1948 and were on their way to another in 1954. It's important to keep in mind that a lot of people liked listening to baseball on the radio. They still do, so it was a real job to move that audience to TV. In fact, a lot of people would watch the game on TV with the sound off and listen to the play-by-play on radio. Ken Coleman was a major force in changing that.

Ken arrived in Cleveland in 1952, and along with his partner, Jimmy Britt, changed the way people watched baseball. They could be compelling without being annoying, and they kept the chatter about anything other than the game to a minimum. They didn't show any phony excitement or bias toward the teams. There was an occasional flub. During one game Ken called a play by the Tribe's Rocky Colavito, saying, "There goes Wally, back against the rock!" That would go on record as one of his few mistakes on the air. Ken would go on to call the action for the Browns, the Indians, and Ohio State during his time in Cleveland. He would always end his broadcast with, "This is Ken Coleman, rounding third and heading home." The legendary Jack Buck called him the greatest football announcer ever, and Ken probably would have stayed if his dream job with the Red Sox hadn't lured him back to Boston.

It wasn't just the announcers. TV also caught up through the efforts of production director Ernie Sindelar and his crew. They sure worked for their money. In 1957 WEWS spent $75,000 on a production truck for the Indians, but it didn't have air conditioning. This was a big truck with a full production studio inside, and that equipment got hot along with the temperatures outside. Sindelar would just strip down to his underwear during the worst days. It's a pretty good guess that there were no female crew members on those shoots.

We mentioned that anything could happen during a live feed, and what the TV audience saw that same year was nothing less than horrifying. It happened on May 7. Herb Score was one of the Indians' rising stars. He was the American League rookie of the year in 1955, and the Indians' general manager, Hank Greenberg, predicted he could become "the greatest pitcher in the game's history." Other teams scrambled to get Herb Score on their rosters. In March of '57 the Red Sox offered a million dollars to the Tribe to buy Score's contract, and they were turned down flat. He was setting records for wins and strikeouts, and it looked as though he was heading for a Hall of Fame career . . . until the night he faced the New York Yankees.

With Score pitching, WEWS was guaranteed a huge audience. The second batter of the night, shortstop Gil McDougal, slammed a line drive back to the mound that hit Score directly in the eye. Score went down with blood streaming from his eye and nose, and he was carried off the field.

Public outcry was overwhelming. More than ten thousand people sent get-well cards and letters, and a fan in California offered to donate an eye! Score was out for the rest of the season, but after three weeks in the hospital he tried to resume his life as best he could. He went ahead with his wedding plans, and that July he walked down the aisle with Nancy McNamara. It was a huge media event. Footage of the wedding right down to the gifts got shipped back to WEWS for that night's news program, and that was quite a feather in the hat for Channel 5. Score and his wife had turned down an offer from NBC-TV's *Bride and Groom* show, which would have given them $6,000 in merchandise and an all-expenses-paid honeymoon in return for exclusive rights. Herb tried to continue in the majors but didn't have the same fire. Five years later Score retired, but he would eventually find work in the broadcast booth calling games.

A lot of different people passed through that broadcast booth at Municipal Stadium. In fact, for a time Ron Penfound was the Indians' booth announcer. People mostly remember the Tribe's radio announcer Jimmy Dudley from his TV spots for the Aluminum Siding Corporation. "Tell 'em Jimmy Dudley sent ya, ya hear?", followed by "Garfield 1-2-3-2-3." But that's not what his partner Bob Neal would hear. Frankly, we couldn't print it!

Few people in broadcasting have despised each other like Jimmy Dudley and Bob Neal. No one is even sure how it started. They did the games on WERE-AM, with Jimmy calling the first three innings, Bob doing the next three, and Jimmy finishing the game. This feud went on for years. It wasn't just during the games, either. Art Shreiber did news at WERE, and he remembered them both as

That's not faked—it's a real photo, and a rare one, too. It was no secret just how much Bob Neal (left) and Jimmy Dudley (right) disliked each other. *Cleveland Press Collection, Cleveland State University Archives*

nice guys . . . as long as you didn't mention the other one. "Jimmy would come in and ask, 'Did that son-of-a-bitch Neal touch any wire copy?! If he did, I don't want it!'" Neal was an easygoing guy as well, but he wouldn't even walk the same halls as Dudley. "I won't breathe the same air as that bastard!"

It was painfully obvious to anyone who knew them. But in August 1959, out of nowhere, the two started to talk to each other on the air. It was a little stiff, but that wasn't the point. It even made headline news. The *Cleveland News* ran an article headlined, "Did Dudley, Neal Bury the Hatchet?" Maurice Van Metre wrote they were seen as silent partners because "words have rarely passed between them while the games have been in progress." But all of a sudden the two seemed to be on speaking terms again, at least during the games. Neal did a speech at the Wigwam Club and said, "Just to prove to our listeners that we are not at swords' point, maybe I can get Jimmy to dance a jig with me in our small announcing booth at the stadium." That would have made quite a picture, but it wasn't going to happen. Pretty soon they were back at each other's throats, and it got so bad that station management sent its promotions director to stand between them during the game. He even went on the road with them. It didn't matter how small the announcer's booth was, he was right in the middle. Years later he recalled, "I would stand there and Jimmy would say, 'Would you ask that horse's ass Neal where the scores are from last night's game!?" Neal was two feet away. "Jimmy needs last night's scores." Neal would snap, "Tell that bastard to open his eyes. I left them at the side of his typewriter!" "They're at the side of the typewriter, Jimmy." "Oh. Thanks."

Nobody at the station really cared for the promotions director. Bob West was at WERE back then and says, "Ray Miller owned the station, and he was the head of the Cuyahoga County Democratic Party. He hired the kid as a favor. He was Adlai Stevenson's nephew." Seeing no future as a buffer between Jimmy Dudley and Bob Neal, he headed to California for a career in network television. His name was McLean Stevenson.

A Groundbreaker

George Anthony Moore

JUST ABOUT ANYONE WHO did any job at the beginning of local television could be considered a pioneer. Everything was new—from the time you switched on a camera to the sign-off for the night. But there were some people behind the scenes who stand out, and George Anthony Moore is front and center.

Cleveland was a far different place when TV first went on the air. Racial segregation was part of everyday life, and George Moore saw it from an early age. He had grown up in the inner city, and his mother stressed the importance of education. When the time came to look for a solid high school with an eye toward college, she tried to enroll George in St. Ignatius. But she was told in no uncertain terms that no Jesuit school in the country admitted black students. It took an appeal to then–Bishop Edward Hoban to get George through the door.

George excelled at St. Ignatius and went on to the Ohio State University to study theater. His roommate was Jesse Owens. When people would ask George what Jesse looked like, he would say, "It depends. When I see him on the track I only see the back of his head!" George went on to get a master's degree at the University of Iowa, and that led to an opportunity in this new thing called television. But there was a stop along the way.

In the 1940s, the news business was pretty much populated by white men, but Louis Seltzer at the *Cleveland Press* saw something he liked in George. He hired him in 1942 at a time when no major newspaper outside New York City had an African American on its staff. It also paid off big-time for Seltzer. George distinguished

George Anthony Moore was a pioneering broadcaster who broke the color barrier long before the civil rights movement of the 1960s. *Cleveland Public Library*

himself as a solid reporter. He won wide acclaim for an investigative series about poor-quality meat being sold in the inner city. He was dedicated, too. George continued to write and finish the story even after he was laid up in the hospital with a leg injury.

Socko Meets His Match

The Dark World of Alan Douglas

CLEVELAND TELEVISION HAD A lot of unique personalities, and Alan Douglas certainly fit that description. He was in Detroit radio for a long time before he hooked up with Bill Randle in Cleveland in the mid-1950s. Douglas looked more like a college professor than a TV personality. He had salt-and-pepper hair and a neatly trimmed gray beard, one of the few people in television with facial hair. He was also extremely reckless.

Douglas worked at a few radio stations in Cleveland before making the move to TV. He welcomed controversy, and sometimes it got him hot water. In 1965 he debuted a show on WEWS that the *Cleveland Press* called "a morning version of *The Tonight Show*." But Douglas was no Johnny Carson, and *The Tonight Show* didn't talk about hot-button topics like Viet Nam and the civil rights movement. It might have scared away the audience. After a year Channel 5 cancelled the show and replaced it with Don Webster's *TV Bingo*. No controversy, and the station could sell a game show.

Douglas still did some free-lance announcing and had radio shows on WKYC and WHK. Shortly after WKBF signed on in 1968, Alan Douglas came on board to do a TV version of his radio talk show. Channel 61 got complaints from the very first show. His first guest was Josiah Thompson, a college professor turned private detective who claimed the Kennedy assassination was a conspiracy. Now keep in mind that this was 1968, and there wasn't a lot of talk about a possible JFK conspiracy at that time. That really didn't kick into high gear until 1974, when Geraldo Rivera showed the unedited Abraham Zapruder film on *Good Night, America*. Douglas's second guest spot was a kid who had been thrown out of the Cleveland schools for the length of his hair. This was when the generation gap was starting to peak, and Douglas took the side of the schools against the parents, who were in support of their son. This was a guy who loved to argue and didn't care who he argued with. There's an old saying that discretion is the better part of valor. Douglas could have used a lot more of the former.

In 1969 he had a biker gang on his TV show, and it didn't go well. After essentially calling them criminals, it turned into a shouting match, and after the show it got even uglier. Fortunately the gang left Douglas with only a beating in the parking lot. It was fortunate because he could have been killed. It was the same act he did on radio. A year later, in August 1970, Douglas started screaming at members of the National Committee to Combat Fascism (NCCF), an arm of the Black Panther party. The NCCF's Norman X, Tommie Carr, and Amo Koea took offense at Douglas's asking, "What do you people want to do for the city?" The show started spiraling around the drain fast. Douglas knew he was out-numbered and brought the show to an abrupt end at 11:30 p.m., blaming a "communications gap." He went to recorded music, but there was a very heated exchange off-mic. Douglas told police the NCCF reps had sworn at him and physically gone after him and his producer, Bill Baker. The cops were called in, but there were no arrests or charges or apologies. Douglas said that "you people" was not meant to be a slur, only a reference to the NCCF, and he wouldn't invite them back. The NCCF was not a group to annoy. Six weeks before the show, a raid on its headquarters at East 79th Street and Rawlings Avenue resulted in gunfire, wounding both a Cleveland policeman and a member of the NCCF.

The *Press*'s Don Robertson got a laugh out of Douglas's bravado. He congratulated Alan "Socko" Douglas and Bill "One Round" Baker in his column. "It was heartening to learn they had defended themselves so vigorously the other night when they allegedly were attacked by several representatives of a group calling itself The National Committee to Combat Fascism. I bet you don't know that Douglas, for one, used to be a professional boxer. His prom-

This is about as happy as Alan Douglas got. He wasn't afraid to confront people on the air, and they returned the favor—often with a fist. *Cleveland Public Library*

ising career was, however, short-lived. His opponents kept taking advantage of him. That beard covered his glass jaw."

Was Douglas looking for a fight? Chances are, he was. The slightest thing could set him off. Years later he was visiting Cleveland and stopped by WERE-AM to be a guest on a talk show. The news anchor, Mike Drexler, was signing off and saw Douglas waiting in the hall, wearing a cowboy hat. He told the audience to stand by for the station's special guest, Roy Rogers. Douglas stormed into the studio throwing punches, but Drexler was built like a fullback. It was a two-hit fight. He hit Douglas in self defense, and Douglas hit the floor. The glass beard shattered once again.

As unpredictable as he was, Douglas never had a problem finding work. He still had his radio show, and in 1970 he even got a daily talk show on Channel 61. It was called *Newsroom: Cleveland Today*. Always looking for controversial guests, Douglas featured a rookie councilman named Dennis Kucinich and his wife, Helen, on the first show. Dennis was making a lot of noise on Cleveland City Council, but Douglas seemed more interested in Kucinich's original plans to be a ventriloquist. Dennis was destined for a much bigger stage.

Life took a drastic turn for Douglas in 1972. Don Perris at Channel 5 had an idea for a talk show, a modern version of the old *One O'Clock Club*. The station took a big jump, cancelling Miss Barbara's *Romper Room* and Paige Palmer's show to make room on the schedule. Douglas was named host with Don Webster as his sidekick, and The *Morning Exchange* premiered on January 3. Tragedy struck two months later. Douglas's son Cameron returned to the family's Sagamore Hills home on the evening of Friday, March 3. Discovering his mother's car missing, he called his father. Barbara Lee Douglas never returned home that night, and they filed a missing persons report at 5 a.m. A few hours later a real estate agent showed up at a model home on Tinker's Lane to set up an open house, opened the garage, and found Barbara Lee Douglas dead in the front seat of her car. The keys were in the ignition but the motor was off, and she was pronounced dead at St. Thomas Hospital in Akron. Summit County coroner A. H. Kyriakedes determined that the forty-eight-year-old woman had died of carbon monoxide poisoning. There was no apparent reason for Barbara Douglas's suicide. She had a successful radio and TV career and gave it up after Cameron was born in 1966. She even worked weekends, filling in for her husband when he did *Nightline* on WERE. It was not likely he would return to WEWS. His replacement was Fred Griffith, who would stay with the show until it went off the air in the 1990s.

Alan Douglas turned in his resignation to WEWS that July to replace "Long John" Nebel at WNBC radio in New York. The staff had its own "Cleveland Clan" with Don Imus, who came from WGAR, and Big Wilson. It wasn't the same Alan Douglas. His

Talk show host Alan Douglas knew how to push his guest's "hot buttons" . . . and too often, they knew how to push back. *Cleveland Press, author's collection*

show never took off. It had no energy, and Douglas was reassigned to an administrative job and an overnight air shift. His replacement was Wolfman Jack. He battled with WNBC for years, even suing them for breach of contract, but without any luck. In 1974 Douglas finally packed his bags for a gig as a night talk-show host at WXYZ in his old hometown, Detroit. On his second night on the job they found his car on Hines Road with Douglas slumped behind the wheel, dead. His wrists were slashed and a bottle of pills was on the passenger seat. The station aired a taped message that said, "Due to circumstances beyond our control, the *Alan Douglas Show* will not be heard" and filled the rest of the time slot with music.

After his death a friend said, "He was in a killer business. Even when you're on top, you can't relax." No one ever remembers Alan Douglas as relaxed.

Hands Off the Untouchables!

The Return of Eliot Ness

ON APRIL 20, 1959, a story with local flavor made it to the networks when the *Westinghouse Desilu Playhouse* aired the first installment of a film based on Eliot Ness and Oscar Fraley's book, *The Untouchables* on WEWS. Ness's widow Betty and their son Robert watched the presentation with friends in Lyndhurst and, though she wasn't married to Ness when he was busting gangsters in Chicago, she was delighted with Robert Stack's characterization of her husband. Ness was Cleveland's safety director from 1935 to 1942, after the *Untouchables* era, and married Betty in 1946. He died just after the book was written, and it didn't sell that well because he couldn't promote it. The series gave new life to paperback sales and presented marketing tie-ins as well. Despite the violent nature of the show, a lot of the marketing was aimed at children, including board games, figurines and toy guns. Even so, TV violence was very much on the minds of Cleveland area parents. So were concerns about stereotyping.

Lots of people have heard the story . . . and legend . . . of Eliot Ness, whose life took on mythical proportions when the book, TV series and movies about "The Untouchables" came out after his death. But few people knew the real Ness like his third wife, Elizabeth (better known as "Betty") and their adopted son, Robert.

Elizabeth Ness had a busy life before she met her future husband. Born in South Dakota, she graduated from the Cleveland School of Art in 1927 and quickly gained recognition as a sculptress, winning four first-place prizes in the prestigious May Show, as well as exhibiting two twelve-foot statues on the grounds of the

The man who helped bring down Al Capone had a tough time in Cleveland, but Eliot Ness became a folk hero when *The Untouchables* made it to TV. *Cleveland Press, author's collection*

Art imitates life . . . sort of. Robert Stack's take on Eliot Ness ignored most of the public and personal turmoil Ness would face during his career. *Cleveland Public Library*

1936 Great Lakes Exposition. Like many other women of the time, she worked during World War II, in a lens-grinding lab and also doing commercial art and later designing military camouflage. Betty married another Cleveland artist named Hugh Seaver and moved to New York to produce commercial sculptures at a studio there. After a time, her marriage to Seaver fell apart, and she met the man who would have a date with destiny, Eliot Ness.

Ness, a serious and private man devoted to public service, was only remotely similar to portrayals by Robert Stack and Kevin Costner. They played him like a superhero, while in real life Ness had the same temptations and downfalls as any normal human being. Despite his many victories, Ness suffered a series of personal and business failures before passing away at the age of fifty-four in 1957 at his home in Coudersport, Pennsylvania. Ness was cremated, and his remains were turned over to Betty and Robert, who soon headed back to Cleveland.

Prior to his death, Ness had completed the manuscript for *The Untouchables* with Oscar Fraley, and while waiting for its publication, he started assembling notes for a possible follow-up about his years in Cleveland, especially the hunt for the "Kingsbury Run" killer. He never lived to see the book become a hit TV series, but his family would be influenced beyond their wildest dreams.

Betty and her son moved to a home on North Park Boulevard in Cleveland Heights, and the pilot film and series hit the air when Bobby was a seventh grader at Roxboro Junior High. Teachers recall Bobby as a quiet boy, who became reclusive when other kids talked about their dads. But when his father came to life in the Desilu series, Bobby became an entirely different person. Betty recalled, "Since the television programs started . . . Bobby's friends and teachers ask him about his father, and he can talk about him. Bobby is so happy!"

Betty took work at Rella's, an upscale boutique at East 105th and Carnegie. There was a promise of royalties from the movie, TV series, and book, as well as the related products, but that would be divided among her, Oscar Fraley, the publisher, and an agent. She received a little less than two hundred dollars for each first-run episode and twenty-eight dollars per rerun, and Betty planned to salt away that money for Bobby's education. She could never have imagined the continuing impact the series and book would have on their lives. The series became an instant hit, prompting Betty to tell a *Cleveland Press* reporter that, "Life was never dull with Eliot when he was alive. Thanks to Eliot, life is still not dull!" She relocated with her son to a home on Overlook Road in Cleveland Heights, and Bobby became a celebrity among his friends. In fact, one of his best friends was an Italian boy, and the two reveled in playing their version of *The Untouchables.*

There was correspondence from around the country, asking if much of the series had been fictionalized (which she freely admitted) and commenting that Eliot should be known all over America.

You Are the Witness! The proposed TV series had guests watch movie clips to check how observant they were. The pilot featured Eliot Ness' widow, Betty (far left). *Author's Collection, Cleveland Press*

Betty even received a note from Robert Stack, who portrayed her late husband, asking if the show met her approval. She got to respond in person when Stack was profiled in an episode of *This Is Your Life*, and Betty came out to congratulate him in person. (Years later, Stack would say it was one of the most humbling and memorable moments of his career.)

While the series was in production, Betty took work as a research coordinator in the gynecology department at University Hospitals. It wasn't long before she was asked to make some appearances on local TV to capitalize on the fame connected with the Ness name. In May 1961, Betty debuted on KYW's *Dimension 3* program in a segment called "You Are The Witness" with the station's Tom Haley, Karamu director Dorothy Silver, and Dr. Bernard Dryer of the Western Reserve Medical School. Host Ronnie Barrett showed the panel movie clips, quizzed them on what they had seen, and then compared their answers by running the scene again. The producers had hoped to sell the show to a network, but it failed to draw widespread interest.

But all was not well at Desilu. While *The Untouchables* was a runaway hit, it also drew the wrath of Italian Americans, including gangster Al Capone's widow Mae and his boy Sonny. Frank Sinatra confronted executive producer Desi Arnaz at a Hollywood club, demanding he stop portraying Italians and Sicilians in such a poor light. Fueled by an evening of alcohol, Arnaz faced off against Sinatra and his "friends," saying he wasn't afraid of them, and mocking the singer by asking, "What should I make them? Cubans?" Cleveland's Italian community wasn't pleased either, threatening to boycott advertisers, and as a result, WEWS became the first station nationwide to drop the show from its schedule. The series celebrating Eliot Ness would not be seen in the town in which he had run for mayor.

Betty was enraged. She shot back at the show's critics, saying, "I have many, many letters from youngsters who want to grow up to be like Eliot. They want to be law enforcers. They don't want to be like gangsters! Let's not pretend that gangsters are not the way they are presented on TV. Eliot often told me how really stupid, cruel, and brutal they are. Actually, they are worse than depicted on TV. Eliot told me stuff that would curl your hair!" She went on to say *The Untouchables* was being singled out because of its popularity, while other far inferior programs were left alone. Betty also blasted the show's opponents, saying they shouldn't stand in the way of a program that helped popularize the police and fighting crime. "If a program can bring out the fact that the good guys win," she said, "this should inspire people to uphold the law. It's something like King Arthur and his Knights of the Round Table." Her words fell on deaf ears. *The Untouchables* was retired from Channel 5's prime-time fare.

A few years passed before the film *Bonnie and Clyde* renewed interest in the gangster era, and Desilu put the show back into syndication. It found its way back onto Cleveland's late-night UHF schedule, and Betty and her son were able to finally see many of the episodes that had never aired on WEWS during their first run. It also ran without the controversy surrounding its first go-round on network TV, winning an even wider range of fans in syndication. But it wouldn't be the last time Betty and Bobby Ness found themselves thrust into the headlines.

Betty moved to San Juan Capistrano, California, in 1972, while Robert got married, relocated downtown and studied electrical engineering at Cleveland State. In April the next year, a woman identifying herself as Elizabeth Katherine Ness, Eliot's reputed fourth wife, came to Cleveland to do research about her alleged unhappy marriage to the legendary lawman, with plans to write a "tell-all" book. Not only that, the woman claimed to have married him twice for a total of six years, claiming he was a womanizer and a heavy drinker who married her for money rather than love. The woman claiming to be the former Mrs. Ness promised to "reveal the vices he destroyed, [that] eventually destroyed him." She also claimed to have known all of the Roosevelt children, and dined on hot dogs with the king and queen of England when they visited Hyde Park. She made it very clear she would be writing the book for profit, but Ness's wife and adopted son weren't about to take her charges lying down.

Both Betty and Bobby denounced the woman as an imposter, with the third Mrs. Ness saying, "Maybe she saw too many of those TV programs and has Eliot mixed up with Robert Stack!" Robert Ness, who was working at Christie Labs at the time, told a *Cleveland Press* reporter, "I'd like to see that woman prove the marriage." He also expressed disbelief that his father's scrapbooks, which he had loaned to the Western Reserve Historical Society, were being used by the woman for her research. Betty also noted that Ness's first two wives were named Edna and Evaline, and said, "The only other Elizabeth Ness I know of appeared in the TV series as a fictitious character." The woman and her story both soon faded away.

Bobby died some time later, in August 1976, and his mother passed away from cancer just a little more than a year after that.

There were still some lingering memories of Eliot Ness, including a fading sign for his failed mayoral bid painted on buildings at Cedar and Union Avenues, but never a gravestone. In 1997, a historian and Ness biographer approached the Cleveland police department and suggested a proper memorial for Eliot, Betty, and their son. On September 10, more than fifty years after he brought Al Capone to justice, Ness and his family were given an official police funeral. A black 1938 Buick carried their remains to Cleveland's Lake View Cemetery, the final resting place of John D. Rockefeller, President James Garfield, and so many others. As bagpipers played "Amazing Grace," the family's ashes were poured from a boat into a small pond at the cemetery, and a memorial stone proclaiming the legend and legacy of one of Cleveland's most famous and even controversial public figures, was unveiled on the shore.

The Cleveland Clan

Local Talent Heads to Hollywood

WHEN TV FIRST HIT the air in Cleveland, it was the seventh-biggest city in the United States. It had a thriving night club scene, and a lot of major talent made its way through town. But then, as now, the big money was in New York and California. Most of the major TV shows were filmed in Los Angeles, and brutal winters up north were a major selling point for heading west. Several talented television professionals from Northeast Ohio eventually set out for the West Coast. They became known as the "Cleveland Clan."

Tim Conway, the first to relocate, came back with stories of big opportunities and big money. Pretty soon it turned into a talent drain for local entertainers. Ray Walston spent time with the Cleveland Playhouse in the mid-1940s before heading to Hollywood, where he would eventually get the lead in *My Favorite Martian*. Jack Riley at WERE took the plunge and started writing for Jerry Van Dyke as well as performing. He'd been doing TV at WEWS with his radio partner Jeff Baxter, but Jeff had too much work in Cleveland to head west. Jack was first seen as a character named Wally Frick on NBC's *Occasional Wife* in 1966, but in 1972 he struck gold playing Elliot Carlin on *The Bob Newhart Show*.

Pat McCormack graduated from Rocky River High School in 1945 and was at Harvard Law School when the acting bug bit him. He was a writer for *Jack Paar, Candid Camera, Get Smart,* and *The Danny Kaye Show* before he started doing sketch comedy on Johnny Carson's *Tonight Show*. Even though he wasn't a native Clevelander, you could count Mike Douglas in that group. He took a role as a THRUSH agent on *The Man from U.N.C.L.E.* and did plenty of guest appearances on *The Hollywood Palace* and other shows. Ann Elder got screen time on *The Wild, Wild West* and *Ben Casey*, and was a writer and featured player on NBC's *Laugh-In*. They might have left for big jobs in Hollywood, but they never forgot their roots in Cleveland. Sometimes they would do it with inside jokes that only folks from Northeast Ohio would understand.

Tim Conway was riding high as Ensign Chuck Parker on ABC's *McHale's Navy* and did a guest spot on NBC's *Sammy Davis, Jr. Show*. In one skit he started dropping names like Ernie Anderson, Jack Riley, and Don Rumbaugh, who produced the *Mike Douglas Show*. On top of that, he used Channel 8's phone number to close the skit, and a wave of calls flooded the switchboard.

But not everything Tim touched turned to gold. He hosted an edgy comedy show on ABC in February 1969 called *Turn-On* that was heavy on sexual innuendo. It was aimed at competing with *Laugh-In* on NBC, and it had that show's producer, George Schlatter, doing the same job for *Turn-On*. There were so many complaints nationwide, with the WEWS switchboard leading the way, that the network canceled it while it was still on the air! In fact, Channel 5 took it off the air after the first eleven minutes! The official announcement that it was canceled didn't come until several days later, when Bristol-Myers pulled its sponsorship. It didn't matter. WEWS was part of a long list of affiliates that told ABC it refused to run another episode.

The next year, in September 1970, Tim starred on *The Tim Conway Comedy Hour* on CBS along with one-time Clevelander McLean Stevenson and a young dancer named Sally Struthers. A few months later she became Gloria Stivic on *All in the Family*, and by 1972 McLean Stevenson was better known as Col. Henry Blake on *M*A*S*H*.

There were plenty of holdouts. Jack Riley tried his hardest to get Linn Sheldon to California. In 1966 he was pitching a series about a small airport and wanted Linn as the air traffic controller. But there was too much work and money in Cleveland for Linn to start from scratch at his age, so he politely declined. It was the same for

Before he found fame as Mr. Carlin on *The Bob Newhart Show*, Jack Riley teamed with his radio partner, Jeff Baxter, to liven up *The One O'Clock Club* on WEWS. It didn't last long; KYW's Mike Douglas soon owned the time slot. *Cleveland Press, author's collection*

"Big Chuck" Schodowski. Tim Conway offered a standing invitation, but Big Chuck had a family and a steady job, so he turned thumbs down, too. Meanwhile, Ernie Anderson had plenty of friends on the West Coast, so he stayed there during October 1966 after taping several Ghoulardi segments. WJW granted him the month's leave so he could join Tim Conway to film a proposed TV series for ABC called *Rango,* centered on a comical Texas Ranger; Anderson was expected to be in at least four of the first ten shows.

It took some time, but Tim finally convinced Ernie Anderson. Ernie was making huge money as a voice-over artist and as Ghoulardi, but in early 1967 he said goodbye to Cleveland to become the highest-paid announcer in history.

Jack Riley was also scheduled for the first episode, and he would host Anderson during his Hollywood stay. Riley's star was starting

After his stint on *McHale's Navy*, Tim Conway took on
a number of comedy roles, including a bumbling Texas
Ranger named Rango. *Cleveland Public Library*

to rise and there was talk of him getting his own series. Conway
was getting guest shots, too, starring as the "Prince of Parma" in a
skit on the *Dean Martin Show*.

Then there was Jack Hanrahan. This is not a pretty story.

Jack was born in Cleveland in 1933 and eventually found he
could write comedy. He started writing cartoons for the *Cleveland
Press*, verses for American Greetings, and even news at WERE. In
1966 he headed to Hollywood with another greeting-card writer
named Phil Hahn, and things started happening quickly. First stop
was Hanna-Barbera, the home of the *Jetsons, Flintstones,* and *Top
Cat.* They did pretty well there, and that led to a gig writing *Get*

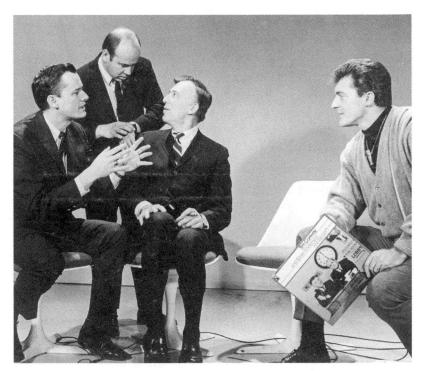

"Are We On?" Ernie Anderson (second from right) ditched Ghoulardi's beard and lab coat to join his old friend Tim Conway (standing) on the west coast. Here, they join Bob "Hoolihan" Wells (left) and "Big Chuck" Schodowski (right) to plug their comedy album. They never got around to talking about the record. *Chuck Schodowski*

Smart. Word got around that Jack and his partner were funny guys, and it wasn't long before they got an offer in November 1967 to write for *Laugh-In*. This is where the story starts to turn.

The writers were looking for a city to make fun of, and all eyes were on Buffalo. Crummy weather, weird name . . . who could ask for more? They started tossing around ideas to crack on Buffalo, and Jack offered one that landed with a thud. Another writer said, "Don't mind Hanrahan. He's from Cleveland!" Light bulbs appeared above their heads. An old rule of comedy is that cities with a hard "C" or "K" sound tend to get laughs. Keokuk, Kokomo, Calabasas, Cleveland. Cincinnati, not so much. Cleveland would be the target, and Jack Hanrahan, whether he liked it or not, became the father of the "Cleveland joke." Phil Hahn later told the *Plain Dealer* that he wrote better than Jack, but Jack was funnier. He was also a great talker and could get his foot in a lot of different doors. He just wasn't very good with details, and there was a reason. When it came to drugs and alcohol, Jack's motto was "Excess is never enough!"

It was a fast life in Los Angeles, and Jack jumped in head first. You saw him at all the parties, and you rarely saw him sober. Jack was also a family man with a wife and six kids. Those two worlds can't co-exist, and Jack Hanrahan found out the hard way. He relocated from Beverly Hills and headed north to Eureka, California, in 1992. He was still getting writing jobs, but shows like *Super Mario World* and *Inspector Gadget* didn't have the prestige or paychecks that he had seen in the past. Jack even starred in a low-budget movie called *Up Your Alley* in 1988. Although able to provide for his family, he was fighting demons, and the demons were winning.

After Jack's wife died in 2004, his life went into a steep decline. He couldn't shake the grief, and the demons kicked into high gear. An old friend told the *Plain Dealer*, "He stopped taking care of himself; he stopped paying his bills and cleaning his house." By 2006 he couldn't pay his rent, and the landlord seized everything in his rented house, including the Emmy. Jack Hanrahan was homeless.

The story gets a little bit sketchy. Jack wanted to start over in Cleveland, and in December 2006 some friends chipped in to get him there. He dropped off his bags in an airport locker but then headed to Ohio on a bus. What few possessions he had were left in that locker, and Jack couldn't remember why he had left them there. Jack's life back in Cleveland started in the winter, and he floated from shelter to shelter, begging money on the streets and going to daily mass at St. John's Cathedral. He was rolling his own cigarettes. He didn't even have teeth. They were left in the locker at Bob Hope Airport in Burbank. Finally, in March 2007, with few if any options, Jack worked up the nerve to call Michael O'Malley at the *Plain Dealer*. "If you want a riches-to-rags story, pal, I've got a good one for you."

The *PD* article helped a lot. He was rediscovered by old friends, who dropped off toiletries and clothes at the homeless shelter. A landlord on the west side gave him an apartment rent-free, and there was even an offer to buy him new dentures. Now, keep in mind that his teeth weren't the only thing he left in California. He came back to Cleveland with nothing, including identification, and that was a big problem. Social workers tried to get Jack mental health counseling, but that couldn't happen without an ID. A member of the Cleveland Clan came to the rescue. Another Jack—Riley—was able to get his military service documents, which opened doors at the Veterans Administration. Riley had come to his aid once before, putting him up at a hotel, but Jack had mysteriously disappeared. He was glad to help when he found Jack was back in Cleveland. The nightmare wasn't over, but it didn't seem as frightening. A follow-up article in the *PD* said that when a VA rep came by to pick Jack up for treatment, he was told, "Don't ever rush the king," and left singing, "Pack up your troubles in your old kit bag and smile, smile, smile . . ." Sadly, there were only a few smiles left.

Jack had heart problems and died in a nursing facility in April 2008, a little over a year after his return to Cleveland. Friends said he knew the end was near, but he always left them with a smile.

"No one believed that I could line up enough guests"

Jim Doney and Adventure Road

TELEVISION OPENED A LOT of windows for many folks who might have never left Northeast Ohio. A good example was Jim Doney's *Adventure Road*. Based on a similar show in Detroit that got a lot of attention, it was basically a travelogue. People would bring in home movies from their trips, and five days a week WJW would give them an opportunity to tell folks about their vacations. The difference between watching at home or on a projector in someone's living room was, you could turn it off when you'd had enough.

Doney had been with the station almost from day one. He was a booth announcer and weekend newscaster for about ten years before the station tapped him for the new show. It went on the air in December 1962, first on the weekends and then, beginning March 1963, six days a week. Now, keep in mind that this was before TV news had come into its own. When *Adventure Road* started its weekday run, it would air from 5:30 to 6:40 p.m. It's anyone's guess why it was such a hit. At first even Doney didn't think it would fly. He told a *Cleveland Press* reporter, "At first I was lukewarm, if even that, about the show." Some folks shared that opinion. Doney went on to say, "WJW wanted the program to run daily from the beginning, but no one believed that I could line up enough guests to do a daily show. After one trip to New York, I had four months of solid bookings." There were a couple of reasons for that. One, people wanted to be on TV. In the days before mobile news cameras you had very little opportunity unless

Jim Doney made his mark on TV by showing other people's home movies. Here he is in Conneaut, although his *Adventure Road* featured vacation films from around the world. *Cleveland Press, author's collection*

you were invited to the studio. Second, you could now pick up cameras that shot eight-millimeter for a reasonable price, and a lot of people used them on their vacations.

Letters started pouring in, and station management started talking about possible syndication. This was based on grainy vacation films! In 1964 it was the first locally produced show to be broadcast in color. The "road" took some weird twists and turns, as well. Word came down that one of the "tour guides" Doney had hosted was a U.S. spy who was later found murdered in the hills of Guatemala.

It wasn't long before Doney himself started gathering film for the show. Before *Adventure Road* he'd never been outside the United States other than a few quick trips to Canada. By 1969 he was logging more than 70,000 miles a year for the show. He even had requests from people who wanted to see where their servicemen sons were stationed. But the writing was on the wall for *Adventure Road*. It had a core audience, but midafternoon game shows brought in a lot more viewers and national ad money. It got moved around the schedule, with its last time slot at 9:30 a.m. Finally, after a twelve-year run, it left the air in May 1975. WJW's general manager Tom Bergeson said the show suffered from an "obvious fatigue factor," but allowed Doney to shop it around to other stations. Doney decided to hit the road himself, moving his family to Hawaii for a TV job on the islands and, eventually, retirement.

Epilogue

WHEN YOU THINK BACK, you realize that the folks in Northeast Ohio were really blessed. It became evident when we were researching this book. There were so many memorable personalities and events in the golden age of television. We got to know many of the pioneers, all of whom were all eager to share memories of those remarkable times. Linn Sheldon stood above them all.

Every visit Janice and I paid Linn and his wife, Laura, was memorable but way too short. Here's a keeper.

On July 10, 2003, Linn's car was in the shop and he gave me a call. "Bank. Grocery store. Lunch. Take me to the first two and I'll take you to the last." Our goddaughter, Bianca Kontra, was seven years old at the time and was staying with us for the day. Linn said, "Bring her along. She can't eat that much!" I drove out to Winton Place, and when he got in on the passenger side I could tell something was wrong. Linn introduced himself to Bianca, looked at me, and said, "Bad news. Clay Conroy passed away this morning." These two guys had had a special chemistry. You thought they could read each other's minds, and that's part of what made them so memorable. The guy who had played Barnaby had told me Woodrow was dead, and Bianca had never gotten to see them in their prime on TV. However, Bianca was always very bright and very aware, and she realized how important Linn was by the number of people who came up throughout the day to say "hello" and shake his hand. Before we said goodbye to Linn she wisely asked "Mr. Sheldon" for his autograph.

Linn always seemed amazed that people would go out of their way to meet him, and he never let them down. He was always on, and would come up with a memorable line at the drop of a hat. One day we were walking through the Cleveland Clinic and a woman in her sixties stopped him to say, "It's so good to see you here!" He didn't blink. "In a *hospital*?"

Linn had hesitated when he was first approached to do local TV in the 1940s. He thought he would never be remembered. By the time he retired in the 1990s, it was obvious he would never be forgotten.

TV was probably primitive at best until the mid-1970s, but that could be why we remember it so well. Television became part of our lives, and the news people and entertainers were part of our families. It was driven by the personalities. People such as Ron Penfound, Clay Conroy, Dorothy Fuldheim, Gene Carroll, Ernie Anderson, and, of course, Linn Sheldon all have a special place in our collective memories that can never be duplicated. They made us laugh and cry—and made some of us wonder how we could be part of that amazing world behind the glass screen.

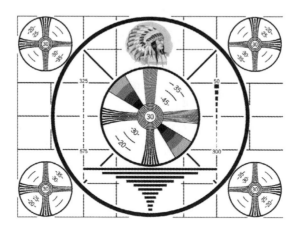

Acknowledgments

Carlo Wolff is one of the best writers in Northeast Ohio and was very generous with his advice and encouragement. He's also a terrific friend. This book would not have been possible without him.

Also, our sincere gratitude to Matt and Cara Penfound, the kids Matthew and Madeline, and the entire Penfound family.

And we can't forget Laura Sheldon Otis and the entire family of our dear friend, Linn Sheldon. The memories we share could fill volumes.

Special thanks also to Chris Andrikanich, Cliff Baechle, Bill Barrow, Bill Becker, Lynn Bycko, Brad Funk, Eric Funk, Rick Funk, David Gray, Jerry Immel, Jeff Jontzen, Bianca Kontra, Tom Kontra, Jim Kraizel, Maureen Kraizel, Jane Lassar, Angelina Leas, Connie Little, Dave Little, Rob Lucas, Candy Lee Korn, Jenny Kingsolver Misciagna, Cate Misciagna, Cole Misciagna, Cora Misciagna, Theresa Misciagna, Tony Misciagna, Dan O'Shannon, Jane Price, Roger Price, George Shuba, Doris Springborn, Althea Sumpter, Noreen Swope, Tom Swope, and Jack Ulman.

Bibliography

Unattributed Articles

"2 New Proposals Due for Community TV." *Cleveland Press,* January 6, 1965.
"Announcer Adair Hikes 23 Miles for Health Fund." *Plain Dealer,* March 11, 1962.
"Betty Cope deplores TV fund veto." *Cleveland Press,* July 1, 1972.
"Bill Gordon May Return to WEWS." *Cleveland Press,* February 26, 1965.
"Bob Dale, Mary Ellen Quit WEWS." *Cleveland Press,* October 4, 1956.
"Carl Stern forces FBI to reveal data." *Cleveland Press,* December 10, 1973.
"Channel 5 top strut all night." *Cleveland Press,* April 29, 1977.
"Channel 8 drops its anchor team." *Cleveland Press,* July 1, 1977.
"Channel 8's Murray Stewart found dead, autopsy set." *Cleveland Press,* August 4, 1976.
"Channel 43 Manager Resigns." *Plain Dealer,* March 31, 1973.
"Ch. 61 economy knife cuts news, Robertson." *Cleveland Press,* November 13, 1970.
"City's Fifth TV Station in Action." *Plain Dealer,* September 15, 1968.
"Channel 61 Has Real Station Break." *Plain Dealer,* January 14, 1968.
"Cleveland TV Stations React." *Cleveland Press,* November 14, 1969.
"Dominic pleads for TV restraint after runaway Moore coverage." *Plain Dealer,* March 10, 1977.
"Doug Adair off the air in strike." *Cleveland Press,* April 1, 1976.
"Driven water Pipe Put Damper on TV in City." *Plain Dealer,* October 6, 1949.
"Ex-reporter for TV station plans bias suit over salary." *Cleveland Press,* November 12, 1970.
"First Public Television Broadcast Here to Offer Press Annual Christmas Show." *Cleveland Press,* December 16, 1947.
"First Telecast Here Huge Success." *Cleveland Press,* December 3, 1947.
"Foreman Uses Shovel at WEWS Ceremony." *Plain Dealer,* March 27, 1947.
"Guthrie, Armstrong Fired by WJW." *Cleveland Press,* August 10, 1963.
"How WEWS Set Stage for Scoop." *Cleveland Press,* August 10, 1965.
"Jorgensen Leaves." *Cleveland Press,* April 2, 1964.
"Linn Sheldon Out as Host of 'Town' Show." *Plain Dealer,* September 23, 1967.
"Mike Douglas Show May Go on WBC Net." *Plain Dealer,* May 21, 1963.
"Murray Stewart found dead in Beachwood motel." *Plain Dealer,* August 4, 1976.
"Murray Stewart took his own life." *Cleveland Press,* August 5, 1976.
"Plot against Akron publisher is foiled." *Cleveland Press,* March 5, 1974.
"Priest asks 'Mary' boycott." *Cleveland Press,* February 5, 1977.

"Put Viewers to Sleep, Keeps 'Em Awake Now." *Cleveland Press,* June 11, 1959.

"Sees Future TV Help Mom to Mind the Baby." *Plain Dealer,* March 26, 1953.

"Sportscaster Jim Graner dies." *Cleveland Press,* January 16, 1976.

"Strikers Vote To Remain Out." *Cleveland Press,* December 24, 1949.

"TV Across the Ocean Predicted for 1980." *Cleveland Press,* October 31, 1956.

"TV Newscaster Says Thinkers use papers." *Cleveland Press,* February 27, 1960.

"TV reporters 'arrested'." *Cleveland Press,* August 31, 1977.

"TV weatherman sues WGAR, disc jockey." *Cleveland Press,* December 9, 1970.

"Union strikes WJW-TV—and pickets WJW Radio." *Cleveland Press,* November 15, 1973.

"WEWS' Bob Dale Going to San Diego for Health." *Plain Dealer,* October 4, 1956.

"WEWS Finds 'See' Legs After Rough Sailing." *Cleveland Press,* November 1, 1948.

"WEWS Team Leaves to Film War in Viet." *Cleveland Press,* December 5, 1967.

"WEWS to Air Local Series on Civil Rights." *Cleveland Press,* March 17, 1961.

"WEWS to Televise Arena Basketball and Hockey Tilts." *Cleveland Press,* November 11, 1948.

"WEWS Will Build 1 1/2 Million Home." *Cleveland Press,* January 25, 1956.

"WJW-TV to add a letter soon" *Plain Dealer,* March 31, 1977.

"WKBF-TV folds, cites financial ills, UHF competition." *Plain Dealer,* April 25, 1975.

"WNBK Seeks to Air Programs of Local Interest." *Cleveland Press,* December 15, 1952.

"WUAB sale set." *Plain Dealer,* July 4, 1977.

"Yanks Refuse WEWS Bid to Televise Game." *Cleveland Press,* September 26, 1949.

Bylined Articles

Adams, Roy W. and Karl R. Burkhardt. "TV Devotes Its Prime Time to Full Coverage of the Killing." *Plain Dealer,* April 6, 1968.

Allen, Forrrest. "Radio Shouldn't Cast Stone in Criticizing Newspapers." *Cleveland Press,* April 21, 1965.

Almond, Peter. "Pinkney reveals Cory and Carter negotiations." *Cleveland Press,* March 9, 1977.

Anderson, Stan. "4 More TV Stations Lined Up for Guthrie's News Program." *Cleveland Press,* July 30, 1951.

———. "East-West All-Star game to Be Carried Here on TV." *Cleveland Press,* December 31, 1953.

———. "Mike of Mike and Buff Fights to Get Back on WEWS." *Cleveland Press,* November 24, 1952.

———. "Third TV Station, WXEL, Opens This Saturday." *Cleveland Press,* December 14, 1949.

———. "WEWS Does Fine Job Showing Witt and Otis in Lincoln Scene." *Cleveland Press,* February 13, 1948.

———. "WEWS to Add Gadget to Sharpen Tribe Telecasts." *Cleveland Press,* May 30, 1956.

Anderson, Stanley. "Cleveland 11th City to Have Television Station." *Cleveland Press,* December 16, 1947.

———. "Decries Critics of Television Who Ignore Modern Audience." *Cleveland Press,* April 1, 1948.

———. "First Ohio Television Program to Be Sponsored by Sohio." *Cleveland Press,* December 10, 1947.

———. "WEWS-FM Begins Broadcasting Tomorrow; on Air to Midnight." *Cleveland Press,* November 26, 1947.

———. "WEWS in Cleveland." *Cleveland Press,* November 14, 1947.

Bacon, Elmore. "Television and Radio." *Cleveland News,* September 6, 1951.

Bailey, Ronald H. "Army Makes TV Newsman Into a Cook." *Plain Dealer,* March 29, 1959.

Barrett, Bill. "After Weeks of Feuding, Jorgensen Leaves KYW-TV." *Cleveland Press,* April 1, 1964.

———. "Another chapter in the saga of the fight for Channel 19." *Cleveland Press,* January 23, 1973.

———. "Doesn't Know What Doug Has, but It's Worth Plenty." *Cleveland Press,* July 16, 1970.

———. "Doug Adair Goes to Ch. 3 in $65,000-a-Year Deal." *Cleveland Press,* July 15, 1970.

———. "Doug says everything's fine." *Cleveland Press,* January 24, 1977.

———. "Here Is the Latest on Fitzgerald and Lund." *Cleveland Press,* July 5, 1966.

———. "Jorgensen Will Ask More Time—or Else." *Cleveland Press,* October 18, 1966.

———. "Lois Works Hard at Being Ragged'. *Cleveland Press,* November 4, 1966.

———. "More to Paige Palmer Than Trimming Tummies." Cleveland Press, March 19, 1965.

———. "Washington Attorney Heads Channel 19 Group, WIXY Says." *Cleveland Press,* July 16, 1968.

Barrett, Bill, and Robert Crater. "Stokes Aids WIXY Fight for Ch. 19." *Cleveland Press,* July 11, 1968.

———. "TV License Holder Challenges 'Out-of-Town' Tag." *Cleveland Press,* July 12, 1968.

Bellamy, Peter. "Ed Fisher, Linn Sheldon are foils for each other in 'Sunshine Boys'." *Plain Dealer,* November 28, 1975.

Bergen, Bus. "TV strikebreakers curbed by court." *Cleveland Press,* November 30, 1973.

Brightman, Esther. "TV's Betty Cope Woman of the Year." *Plain Dealer,* March 25, 1971.

Carter, Janice. "Recipe for longevity." *Plain Dealer,* June 24, 1979.

Chernin, Donna. "The bard of broadcast." *Plain Dealer,* January 17, 1986.

Chudzik, Barbara. "Actor keyed up about Mr. Jingeling." *Cleveland Press,* December 21, 1981.

Collier, Joe. "Jorgensen Was 'Sick for Three Days.'" *Cleveland Press,* August 13, 1965.

Condon, George E. "Chink in TV Armor Is Weak Film Programs." *Plain Dealer,*
    November 2, 1956.
———. "The Day Our Lives Changed." *Plain Dealer,* December 17, 1967.
———. "Haley's Shifty TV Camera Catches City by Surprise." *Plain Dealer,* June 9,
    1956.
———. "Start of Work on New WEWS Home Recalls Memories of TV's Birth Here."
    Plain Dealer, March 27, 1956.
———. "TV Station WXEL Staff Has Opening Night Tingle—Debut Still Six Days
    Away." *Plain Dealer,* December 12, 1949.
———. "WEWS Celebrating 10th Year." *Plain Dealer,* December 17, 1957.
DeCrane, Ray. "Toddlers Spur Success." *Cleveland Press,* January 17, 1969.
Dolgan, Bob. "Did Channel 3 seek Mueller?" *Cleveland Press,* December 31, 1977.
Epperson, J. B. "WEWS Picks Up TV Signals From Antenna in Parma." *Plain Dealer,*
    October 31, 1948.
Feagler, Dick. "Betty Cope Is Channel 25's Woman on Horseback." *Cleveland Press,*
    February 15, 1965.
———. "Nuts discover television." *Cleveland Press,* March 9, 1977.
Flanagan, James B. "Guthrie to Join Sohio PR Staff." *Plain Dealer,* October 22,
    1963.
———. "Paul Sciria Moves From Street to WKYC Studio." *Plain Dealer,* January 8,
    1967.
———. "Son's Death Made Bigger Man of Channel 8's Stewart." *Plain Dealer,*
    December 17, 1967.
Frankel, Jim. "Alan Douglas Again to Give Cleveland Live Video Show." *Cleveland
    Press,* March 5, 1957.
———. "Aussie Finds Cleveland Has Ideas for Down Under." *Cleveland Press,*
    January 10, 1957.
———. "Battle Over Pay Television Is Industry's Hottest Issue." *Cleveland Press,*
    July 1, 1957.
———. "Bill Gordon Goes on TV in 5-Minute Nightly Spot." *Cleveland Press,* April
    26, 1957.
———. "Dorothy Fuldheim, Larry Spivak have Fun Questioning Each Other." *Cleve-
    land Press,* April 18, 1957.
———. "Douglas Receives Nice Plugs, So They Say, But Far Away." *Cleveland Press,*
    May 29, 1962.
———. "Eliot Ness' Capone Drama Wins Approval of Widow." *Cleveland Press,* April
    21, 1958.
———. "Haley's Open Cameras Doing Good Work On Local Level." *Cleveland Press,*
    March 19, 1957.
———. "Just Mourning the Passing of KYW's Morning Surprise." *Cleveland Press,*
    January 31, 1957.
———. "KYW Thanksgiving Special About Pilgrims Is a Novelty." *Cleveland Press,*
    November 22, 1962.
———. "Merchants See Red as Survey on Color Video Displeases." *Cleveland Press,*
    June 19, 1957.
———. "Mike Douglas Overcomes Setbacks in His First Show." *Cleveland Press,*
    December 12, 1961.

———. "Moving of WEWS Puts End to Pioneer TV Era Here." *Cleveland Press,* February 15, 1957.

———. "On Educational TV: Its Challenge, Rewards." *Cleveland Press,* May 22, 1958.

———. "Original TV Program Ideas Still Mostly a Dream Here." *Cleveland Press,* December 11, 1957.

———. "Radio Is Bettering Position in TV Areas, Survey Show." *Cleveland Press,* December 19, 1953.

———. "Raps Union for Blocking Douglas Show Syndication." *Cleveland Press,* May 30, 1963.

———. "TV Develops 'Truth Box' to Get Reliable Ratings." *Cleveland Press,* June 13, 1957.

———. "Two Surveys Here reveal Disquieting Facts on TV." *Cleveland Press,* July 11, 1958.

———. "WEWS Honored for Serving City." *Cleveland Press,* December 14, 1957.

Furcron, Vel. "Is Your TV Weatherman All Wet?" *Cleveland Magazine,* November, 1974.

Gallagher, Nancy. "Blind for 17 Years, Leads Others on TV." *Cleveland Press,* December 8, 1956.

———. "Finds European TV Shuns Women." *Cleveland Press,* June 1, 1957.

———. "Gets Behind Camera for New Angle on TV." *Cleveland Press,* February 2, 1957.

———. "Hunt Teen-Age Talent for WJW-TV Series." *Cleveland Press,* December 14, 1958.

———. "Inside Track to Santa Held by Higg and Bee." *Cleveland Press,* December 22, 1956.

———. "KYW Joins Film Setup to Make 'Casey Jones'." *Cleveland Press,* June 14, 1957.

———. "Lamppost Lighted Way for Del Thomas." *Cleveland Press,* July 7, 1956.

———. "'Miss Barbara' Wins Romper Room Job." *Cleveland Press,* May 2, 1958.

———. "New KYW Newsman Does Own 'Leg' Work." *Cleveland Press,* October 10, 1957.

———. "Paige Palmer Marks 10th Birthday (on TV)." *Cleveland Press,* January 13, 1959.

———. "Tom Haley Is Happiest Working With People." *Cleveland Press,* December 27, 1957.

———. "TV Sets Without Picture Being Built for Sightless." *Cleveland Press,* August 16, 1957.

———. "WEWS Director Hailed for Imagination in TV." *Cleveland Press,* October 5, 1956.

Gluszek, Richard A. "TV newscaster is a pro on both sides of the lens." *Plain Dealer,* March 3, 1974.

Hanrahan, James. "WEWS—A Tribute to E.W. Scripps." *Cleveland Press,* December 16, 1947.

Hart, Raymond P. "Another Hambrick due here." *Plain Dealer,* July 7, 1977.

———. "Bud Dancy 'back home' to talk of love for Berlin and his work." *Plain Dealer,* January 15, 1975.

————. "Cancellation is likely for 'Adventure Road'." *Plain Dealer,* April 5, 1975.

————. "Castiglione, McLeod at mike." *Plain Dealer,* February 15, 1979.

————. "Channel 3 news dumps Paul Sciria." *Plain Dealer,* March 9, 1974.

————. "Ch. 3's Guthrie Awaits School Bell." *Plain Dealer,* July 27, 1969.

————. "Channel 8 crew moves into new quarters." *Plain Dealer,* November 2, 1975.

————. "Channel 61 to go off air." *Plain Dealer,* April 9, 1975.

————. "Doney returns on film to chat about polkas." *Plain Dealer,* May 21, 1977.

————. "Fifth TV station could be successful." *Plain Dealer,* May 16, 1976.

————. "Former Clevelander Perkins Deserves an Olympics Medal." *Plain Dealer,* February 7, 1972.

————. "Ghoulardi Returns for Evening of Fun." *Plain Dealer,* August 13, 1970.

————. "Landess is out, Adair returns." *Plain Dealer,* June 25, 1977.

————. "Linn Sheldon Show Aims at Preschoolers." *Plain Dealer,* March 8, 1971.

————. "Meet Local Television Stations' Unsung Heroes." *Plain Dealer,* June 10, 1973.

————. "Newshawks will spend Yule out of their nests." *Plain Dealer,* December 24, 1978.

————. "Radio Offer Concludes Penfound's Career Here." *Plain Dealer,* May 13, 1972.

————. "That interview: Dorothy Fuldheim stands by it." *Plain Dealer,* December 15, 1976.

————. "The Then 'Romper Room' Fans Are Now GIs as It Endures." *Plain Dealer,* April 19, 1971.

————. "We're Here to Stay', Channel 61 General Manager says." *Plain Dealer,* November 22, 1970.

————. "Will Sheldon Fade From Local TV?" *Plain Dealer,* October 19, 1969.

————. "WJW-TV Seeking Adair Replacement." *Plain Dealer,* July 16, 1970.

————. "Zames Files $600,000 Suit Against WGAR." *Plain Dealer,* December 9, 1970.

Hickey, William. "Blonde brain returns home." *Plain Dealer,* September 1, 1977.

————. "Channel 61's seven year UHF effort hit only fool's gold." *Plain Dealer*, April 20, 1975.

————. "For Pete's Sake! TV-3 is taking on Franklin to clobber the competition." *Plain Dealer,* October 27, 1975.

————. "Hambrick says his farewells; he'll be sorely missed here." *Plain Dealer,* May 31, 1975.

————. "Lobo defends the news on 3." *Plain Dealer,* November 28, 1976.

————. "Newsman on the spot, and the questions posed." *Plain Dealer,* March 9, 1977.

————. "WEWS" *Plain Dealer,* December 11, 1977.

————. "WJW-TV loses battle of 'Mary Hartman'." *Plain Dealer,* March 29, 1977.

————. "WKBF Cancels Its 10 p.m. Newscast." *Plain Dealer,* November 13, 1970.

Jorgensen, Bill. "Swept Off Six Times, Weary Sailor Reveals." *Cleveland Press,* August 10, 1965.

Kane, Russell W. "WEWS, 14 Today, Has Sparkling Past." *Plain Dealer,* December 17, 1960.

Krawchuck, Julian. "Dorothy Fuldheim Fumes Over Rubin." *Cleveland Press,* April 11, 1970.

Lebovitz, Hal. "Most Sports Promoters Undecided on Television." *Cleveland News,* October 29, 1948.

Lucas, Jim. "WGAR Man Freed, Tells of POW Life." *Cleveland Press,* August 31, 1953.

Macdonald, Helen. "Says TV Can Knit Family Tie." *Cleveland Press,* December 15, 1952.

Maharidge, Dale. "The guy with the pointed ears." *Plain Dealer,* November 13, 1977.

Marx, Frank. "History of Television Dates Back to 1873." *Plain Dealer,* December 18, 1949.

McCauley, Regis. "Mel Allen Named Tribe's TV Voice to Replace Score." *Cleveland Press,* February 26, 1968.

McCormick, John. "Lend Eye, Too, New Station Asks of City's Radio Fans." *Cleveland News,* October 29, 1948.

Miller, W. C. "The elf trap - Life won't let Sheldon shed Barnaby." *Plain Dealer,* November 15, 1981.

Minch, John. "Jim Doney Leads 'Walter Mitty' Life." *Plain Dealer,* August 19, 1965.

O'Connell, Tom. "Guthrie Thrives on Busy Schedule." *Plain Dealer,* May 5, 1958.

Peters, Harriet. "Adair is removed as TV anchorman." *Cleveland Press,* August 26, 1972.

———. "Doney at Top Speed on Adventure Road." *Cleveland Press,* April 17, 1963.

———. "Is TV 8 seeking to replace Jim Mueller?" *Cleveland Press,* February 3, 1981.

Plagenz, George. "Adair to preach for hunger relief." *Cleveland Press,* March 8, 1976.

Quinn, Thomas J. "Bud Dancy is Promoted to Network." *Plain Dealer,* March 6, 1966.

Reesing, Bert J. "Ace Newsmen Daly and Adair Mark Banner Year on Channel 8." *Plain Dealer,* September 6, 1964.

Reesing, Bert J. "Ken Bass Recalls Early Polka Days." *Plain Dealer,* June 14, 1967.

———. "Perkins Will Join Huntley, Brinkley." *Plain Dealer,* August 2, 1967.

Robertson, Don. "Channel 61 is dead." *Cleveland Press,* April 14,1975.

———. "Congratulations to Socko Douglas." *Cleveland Press,* August 20, 1970.

———. "To Murray Stewart." *Cleveland Press,* August 9, 1976.

———. "Welcome back, Virgil." *Cleveland Press,* March 14, 1977.

———. "We Need More John Sloweys." *Cleveland Press,* April 20, 1970.

Schneider, Charles. "First Public Television Broadcast Here to Offer Press Annual Christmas Show." *Cleveland Press,* December 16, 1947.

Schuster, Marjorie. "Betty Cope Named ETV Manager, Will Ask FCC for Another Channel." *Cleveland Press,* October 5, 1965.

Seifullah, Alan A. A., and Mary Strassmeyer. "Dorothy Fuldheim, TV news legend, dies." *Plain Dealer,* November 4, 1989.

Seltzer, Louis B. "City's First Television Station Opens the Door to Tomorrow." *Cleveland Press,* December 16, 1947.

Spencer, Robert. "WNBK Manager Says TV to Cover All Phases of Life." *Cleveland News,* October 29, 1948.

Stephan, Robert S. "WNBK Is Newest in TV Field Here; An NBC Auxiliary." *Plain Dealer,* October 31, 1948.

Stranahan, Susan. "Indians Rare Triple Play Is Marred for TV Viewers." *Plain Dealer,* August 10, 1970.

Tittle, Diana. "Can Betty Cope Make Channel 25 a Star?." *Cleveland Magazine,* October, 1977.

Van Metre, Maurice. "Baseball vs. Bishop." *Cleveland News,* May 4, 1953.

———. "Best Radio-TV Shows Given Awards." *Cleveland News,* March 1, 1956.

———. "Did Dudley, Neal Bury the Hatchet?." *Cleveland News,* August 12, 1959.

———. "Field Plays Cupid." *Cleveland News,* August 1, 1957.

Vincent, Beatrice. "Betty Cope Fills TV Director Job." *Cleveland Press,* August 6, 1953.

Warfel, Jack. "Lawson Deming Keeps Smiling for WNBK's Mid-Day Movies." *Cleveland Press,* December 9, 1952.

———. "Warren Guthrie to Start Health Series on WXEL." *Cleveland Press,* December 8, 1952.

Wical, Noel. "Warren Guthrie - Sohio's Best-Known Voice." *Sohioan,* February, 1960.

Books

Douglas, Mike. *Mike Douglas: My Story.* G.P. Putnam's Sons, 1978.

Love, John F. *McDonald's - Behind the Arches.* Bantam Books, 1995.

Television Specials

WEWS-TV. "WEWS—The First Fifty Years" (1997)

WKYC-TV. "35 Great Years" (1983)

WKYC-TV. "Channel 3's Golden Years" (1998)

OTHER BOOKS OF INTEREST . . .

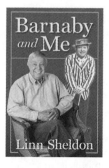

Barnaby and Me
Linn Sheldon

Pioneering children's TV host Linn Sheldon shares his own extraordinary life story. From a Dickensian childhood in Norwalk, Ohio, to Hollywood and back, Sheldon's odyssey includes celebrity, personal tragedy and self-destruction, recovery, and reflection. A remarkable mix of melancholy, hilarity, irony, and warmth.

"A revealing and hilarious look at [Sheldon's] career, which blossomed along with TV itself. The anecdotes are endless." – Sun Newspapers

Ghoulardi
Inside Cleveland TV's Wildest Ride

Tom Feran, R. D. Heldenfels

The behind-the-scenes story of the outrageous Ghoulardi show and its unusual creator, Ernie Anderson. The groundbreaking late-night TV horror host shocked and delighted Northeast Ohio in the mid-1960s on Friday nights with strange beatnik humor, bad movies, and innovative sight gags. Includes rare photos, interviews, transcripts, and trivia.

"Captures a hint of the mania that made Ghoulardi a Cleveland idol in a sleepy era before long hair, drugs, assassinations, war and protests." – Columbus Dispatch

Big Chuck!
My Favorite Stories from 47 Years on Cleveland TV

Chuck Schodowski, Tom Feran

A beloved Cleveland TV legend tells funny and surprising stories from a lifetime in television. "Big Chuck" collaborated with Ernie Anderson on the groundbreaking "Ghoulardi" show and continued to host a late-night show across four decades—the longest such run in TV history. Packed with behind-the-scenes details about TV and celebrities.

"A vivid picture of an honest man in the insane world of television. Highly recommended." – Midwest Book Review

Read samples at **www.grayco.com**

OTHER BOOKS OF INTEREST . . .

Crazy, With the Papers to Prove It
Stories About the Most Unusual, Eccentric and Outlandish People I've Known in 45 Years as a Sports Journalist

Dan Coughlin

An award-winning Cleveland sports reporter tells stories about eccentric and outlandish characters he knew in his 40-year career, including a degenerate gambler; a sportswriter who ripped open beer cans with his teeth; an Olympic champion who turned out to be a hermaphrodite; a football player who was a compulsive practical joker; and many others.

"Fascinating and fun . . . If you love Cleveland sports—in spite of the records—you will love this book." – The Morning Journal

Six Inches of Partly Cloudy
Cleveland's Legendary TV Meteorologist Takes on Everything—and More

Dick Goddard

Legendary Cleveland TV personality and pioneering meteorologist Dick Goddard celebrates 50 years on television with this grab-bag of personal stories, witty cartoons, fun facts, and essays about weather, pets, Ohio history, the TV business, and much more. Includes favorite stories about Dick told by friends and colleagues. Dozens of photos.

The Buzzard
Inside the Glory Days of WMMS and Cleveland Rock Radio—A Memoir

John Gorman, Tom Feran

This rock and roll radio memoir goes behind the scenes at the nation's hottest station during FM's heyday, from 1973 to 1986. It was a wild and creative time. John Gorman and a small band of true believers remade rock radio while Cleveland staked its claim as the "Rock and Roll Capital." Filled with juicy insider details.

"Gorman describes in exclusive, behind-the-scenes detail the state of rock 'n' roll from the early '70s to the late '80s, when just about anything happened and everyone looked the other way . . . Essential reading for musicians, entertainment industry leaders, and music fans." – Mike Shea, CEO/Co-Founder, Alternative Press magazine

Read samples at **www.grayco.com**

OTHER BOOKS OF INTEREST . . .

Cleveland Rock and Roll Memories
True and Tall Tales of the Glory Days, Told by Musicians, DJs, Promoters, and Fans Who Made the Scene in the '60s, '70s, and '80s

Carlo Wolff

Clevelanders who grew up with Rock and Roll in the 1960s, '70s, and '80s remember a golden age, with clubs like the Agora, trendsetting radio stations WIXY 1260 and WMMS, Coffee Break Concerts, The World Series of Rock. Includes first-person stories by fans, musicians, DJs, reporters, club owners, and more, with rare photos and memorabilia.

Cleveland Summertime Memories
A Warm Look Back

Gail Ghetia Bellamy

What made the summertime special to a Cleveland kid? Building sandcastles in your clam diggers at Edgewater Park. Pulling up to Manners Big Boy in your parents' car for a burger and a Big Ghoulardi. An ornate sundae at Boukair's. Watching the Indians lose (again) at Municipal Stadium. Being terrified by Laughing Sal at Euclid Beach Park. And more!

Cleveland Christmas Memories
Looking Back at Holidays Past

Gail Ghetia Bellamy

What made Christmas extra-special to a Cleveland kid? Relive some of your fondest memories: A visit to Mr. Jingeling at Halle's; gazing at the giant Sterling-Lindner-Davis tree; the long line to see Santa at Higbee's—followed by a Frosty; a concert at Severance Hall; mouthwatering treats from Hough Bakery; lights at GE's Nela Park; and more.

Read samples at **www.grayco.com**

OTHER BOOKS OF INTEREST . . .

Cleveland Amusement Park Memories
A Nostalgic Look Back at Euclid Beach Park, Puritas Springs Park, Geauga Lake Park, and Other Classic Parks

David & Diane Francis

Northeast Ohioans who grew up visiting amusement parks in the 1940s through 1970s will cherish the memories and memorabilia captured in this vivid, nostalgic portrait of days gone by. Includes: Euclid Beach Park, Luna Park, Geauga Lake Park, Puritas Springs Park, White City, Memphis Kiddie Park, Geneva-on-the-Lake, and others.

A Touch of Cleveland History
Stories from the First 200 Years

Bob Rich

These 57 short stories are an entertaining introduction to the history of Cleveland, Ohio, for natives or newcomers. They highlight exceptional people and notable events from log cabin days to the mighty industrial era, and cover subjects from sports to fashion to crime. For any Clevelander who wants to know a little more about the old hometown.

Tales from the Road
Memoirs from a Lifetime of Ohio Travel, Television, and More

Neil Zurcher

After a million miles and four decades as a TV reporter, Neil Zurcher has many great stories to tell: He met Prince Charles in a bathroom, and tripped and fell on President Gerald Ford. He raced on an elephant, piloted a glider, and hung from a trapeze. He survived a hotel fire, a tornado, and countless stunts for the camera. Fun tales well told.

"A sparkling gem of a book . . . Intermingled with the pratfalls, hijinks and practical jokes are bittersweet stories of love and romance, tragedy and triumph . . . a remarkably well-written book." – The Morning Journal

Read samples at **www.grayco.com**